Knight Surname

Ireland: 1600s to 1900s

From Ireland Church Records of Baptism, Marriage and Death

Comprised of Roman Catholic and Church of Ireland Records

From Counties Carlow, Cork, Kerry and Dublin City

Compiled by **Donovan Hurst**

March 12, 2012

ISBN: 0985134372
ISBN-13: 978-0-9851343-7-2

Dedication

This work is dedicated to all of those that came before us and shaped our lives to make us the people that we are today.

Table of Contents

Introduction

This is a compilation of individuals who have the surname of Knight that lived in the country of Ireland from the 1600s to the 1900s. I have placed each entry into one of four categories: Families, Individual Births/Baptisms, Individual Burials, and Individual Marriages. If a marriage entry primarily concerns an Individual Knight who is female, then I have placed that entry under the category of Individual Marriages. If a marriage entry primarily concerns an Individual Knight who is male, then I have placed that entry under the category of Families. Images of many of these listings are available at http://churchrecords.irishgenealogy.ie/churchrecords/.

To help guide the reader of this work, the format of this book is as follows:

- Main Family Entry (Husband and Wife) (Father and Mother)

  o Child of Main Family Entry, including Spouse(s) when available

    ▪ Grandchild of Main Family Entry, including Spouse(s) when available

      • Great-Grandchild of Main Family Entry, including Spouse(s) when available

(**Bolded Text**) following any entry includes any additional information such as Residence(s), Occupation(s), Signature(s), etc. when available.

Hurst

Some of the fonts used in this work symbolizes Celtic writing. The traditional letters, numbers, and punctuation marks and their Celtic counterparts are as follows:

Traditional Letters (Uppercase & Lowercase)

A a B b C c D d E f G g H h I i J j K k L l M m N n O o P p Q q R r S s T t U u V v W w X x Y y Z z

Celtic Letters (Uppercase & Lowercase)

A a B b C c D ð E e F ꝼ G g H h I í J j K k L l M m

N n O o P p Q q R ʀ S s T t U u V ʋ W ω X x Y ẏ Z z

Traditional Numbers

1 2 3 4 5 6 7 8 9 10

Celtic Numbers

1 2 3 4 5 6 7 8 9 10

Traditional Punctuation

. , : ' " & - ( )

Celtic Punctuation

. , : ' " & - ( )

Parish Churches
Carlow

Carlow Parish and Dunleckney Parish.

Cork & Ross
[Roman Catholic or RC]

Ardfield & Rathbarry Parish, Bandon Parish, Bantry Parish, Cork - South Parish, Cork - SS. Peter & Paul Parish, Courcy's Country or Ballinspittal Parish, Douglas Parish, Innishannon Parish, Kilbrittain Parish, Kilbrittain & Rathclareen Parish, Kilmacabea Parish, Kinsale Parish, Murragh & Templemartin Parish, and Skibbereen (Creagh & Sullon) Parish.

Dublin (Church of Ireland)

Arbour Hill Barracks Parish, Chapelizod Parish, Clontarf Parish, Glasnevin Parish, Irishtown Parish, Kilmainham Parish, Leeson Park Parish, North Strand Parish, Pigeon House Fort Parish, Portobello Barracks Parish, Rathmines Parish, Rotunda Chapel Parish, Sanford Parish, South Dublin Union Parish, St. Andrew Parish, St. Anne Parish, St. Audoen Parish, St. Barnabas Parish, St. Bride Parish, St. Catherine Parish, St. George Parish, St. James Parish, St. John Parish, St. Luke Parish, St. Mark Parish, St. Mary Parish, St. Matthew Parish, St. Michael Parish, St. Michan Parish, St. Nicholas Within Parish, St. Nicholas Without Parish, St. Patrick Parish, St. Paul Parish, St. Peter Parish, St. Stephen Parish, St. Thomas Parish, St. Victor Parish, St. Werburgh Parish, and Taney Parish.

Dublin (Roman Catholic or RC)

Chapelizod Parish, Harrington Street Parish, Palmerstown Parish, Rathmines Parish, Sandyford Parish, SS. Michael & John Parish, St. Andrew Parish, St. Audoen Parish, St. Catherine Parish, St. James Parish, St. Joseph Parish, St. Lawrence Parish, St. Mary, Donnybrook Parish, St. Mary, Haddington Road Parish, St. Mary, Pro Cathedral Parish, St. Michan Parish, and St. Nicholas Parish.

Knight Surname Ireland: 1600s to 1900s

Kerry (Church of Ireland)

Ballyheigue Parish, Ballymacelligott Parish, Castleisland Parish, Dingle Parish, and Tralee Parish.

Kerry (Roman Catholic or RC)

Ballylongford Parish, Boherbue Parish, Caherciveen Parish, Castleisland Parish, Castletownbere Parish, Killarney Parish, Listowel Parish, and Tralee Parish.

Families

- Abraham Knight & Elizabeth Unknown

  o Mary Knight – bapt. 19 May 1752 (Baptism, **St. Catherine Parish**)

  o Robert Knight – bapt. 8 Jun 1755 (Baptism, **St. Catherine Parish**)

  o William Knight – bapt. 17 Feb 1757 (Baptism, **St. Catherine Parish**)

  o Jacob Knight – bapt. 11 Mar 1762 (Baptism, **St. Catherine Parish**)

- Alexander Knight & Bridget Knight

  o John Knight – bapt. 6 Jan 1696 (Baptism, **St. Michan Parish**)

Alexander Knight (father):

Occupation - Pewterer - January 6, 1696

- Alexander Knight & Mary Knight

  o John Knight – bur. 20 Feb 1697 (Burial, **St. Michan Parish**)

Alexander Knight (father):

Occupation - Castermonger - February 20, 1697

- Alfred Knight & Unknown

  o Harold Christopher Knight & Anne Byrne (B y r n e) – 31 Dec 1898 (Marriage, **St.**

  Catherine Parish)

Signatures:

Hurst

Harold Christopher Knight (son):

    Residence - Portobello Barracks - December 31, 1898

    Occupation - Corporal Rifle Brigade - December 31, 1898

Anne Byrne, daughter of Peter Byrne (daughter-in-law):

    Residence - Cock Street Hospital - December 31, 1898

Peter Byrne (father):

    Occupation - Tailor

Alfred Knight (father):

    Occupation - Carriage Painter

- Ambrose Knight & Frances Knight

  - Isabel Frances Knight – b. 26 Oct 1891, bapt. 14 Oct 1892 (Baptism, **St. Mark Parish**)

  - Herbert Knight – b. 29 Mar 1899, bapt. 31 Jul 1899 (Baptism, **St. Victor Parish**)

Ambrose Knight (father):

    Residence - 20 South Cumberland Street - October 14, 1892

        13A Upper Clanbrassil Street - March 29, 1899

    Occupation - Seeds Man & Florist - October 14, 1892

        Nursery Man - March 29, 1899

- Barnabas (B a r n a b a s) Knight & Sarah Unknown

  - John Knight – bapt. 2 Jul 1727 (Baptism, **St. Nicholas Without Parish**)

  - Mary Knight – bapt. 1 Mar 1730 (Baptism, **St. Nicholas Without Parish**)

Barnabas Knight (father):

    Residence - Hanover Lane - July 2, 1727

        Hanover Row - March 1, 1730

- Charles Knight & Ellen Corcoran

  - Mary Knight – bapt. 6 Apr 1788 (Baptism, **Bantry Parish (RC)**)

Knight Surname Ireland: 1600s to 1900s

- Charles Knight & Margaret Foley – 25 Jan 1801 (Marriage, **Cork - South Parish (RC)**)

Charles Knight (husband):

    Residence - Bandon Road - January 25, 1801

    Relationship Status at Marriage - widower

Margaret Foley (wife):

    Residence - Cove Street - January 25, 1801

    Relationship Status at Marriage - widow

- Charles Frederick Knight & Marion Isabel Knight

  - Bithia Violet Knight – b. 26 May 1877, bapt. 19 Jul 1877 (Baptism, **St. Peter Parish**)

  - William Edwin Knight – b. 28 Mar 1879, bapt. 5 Aug 1879 (Baptism, **St. Peter Parish**)

  - Hubert Artley Knight – b. 15 May 1880, bapt. 20 Jul 1880 (Baptism, **St. Peter Parish**)

  - Charles Frederick Knight – b. 9 Aug 1882, bapt. 5 Sep 1882 (Baptism, **St. Peter Parish**)

  - Queenie Ellice Cornelia Frances Knight – b. 5 Apr 1885, bapt. 25 Aug 1885 (Baptism, **St. Peter Parish**)

  - Alfred Percival Knight – b. 13 May 1886, bapt. 16 May 1886 (Baptism, **St. Peter Parish**)

  - Barbara Victoria Alberta Christina French Knight – b. 28 Oct 1887, bapt. 3 Nov 1887 (Baptism, **St. Peter Parish**)

Charles Frederick Knight (father):

    Residence - 52 Synge Street - July 19, 1877

        56 Synge Street - August 5, 1879

        91 Harcourt Street - July 20, 1880

                September 5, 1882

        82 Harcourt Street - August 25, 1885

        19 Grantham Street - May 16, 1886

        51 Harcourt Street - November 3, 1887

Occupation - Unclear - July 19, 1877

M. D. - August 5, 1879

July 20, 1880

September 5, 1882

August 25, 1885

May 16, 1886

Physician & Surgeon - November 3, 1887

- Christopher Knight & Ellen Reynolds

  o Anthony Knight – b. 28 Dec 1886, bapt. 30 Dec 1886 (Baptism, **SS. Michael & John Parish (RC)**)

  o Mary Knight – b. 18 Jun 1888, bapt. 28 Jun 1888 (Baptism, **SS. Michael & John Parish (RC)**)

  o William Thomas Knight – b. 9 Aug 1889, bapt. 19 Aug 1889 (Baptism, **SS. Michael & John Parish (RC)**)

  o Ellen Christina Knight – b. 3 Dec 1891, bapt. 7 Dec 1891 (Baptism, **SS. Michael & John Parish (RC)**)

Christopher Knight (father):

Residence - 20 Aungier Street - December 30, 1886

7 Digges Street - June 28, 1888

12 Longford Street - August 19, 1889

December 7, 1891

- Christopher Knight & Ellen Weeks – 3 Mar 1772 (Marriage, **St. Audoen Parish**)

- Christopher Knight & Sarah Farmer – 19 Feb 1753 (Marriage, **St. Nicholas Without Parish**)

Christopher Knight (husband):

Occupation - Weaver - February 19, 1753

Sarah Farmer (wife):

Relationship Status at Marriage - widow

Knight Surname Ireland: 1600s to 1900s

- Christopher Knight, d. Before 26 Jul 1858 & Unknown

  o William Knight & Sarah Jane Jones – 26 Jul 1858 (Marriage, St. Andrew Parish)

Signatures:

William Knight (son):

    Residence - No 70 South George's Street - July 26, 1858

    Occupation - Merchant's Assistant - July 26, 1858

Sarah Jane Jones, daughter of Thomas Jones (daughter-in-law):

    Residence - No 70 South George's Street - July 26, 1858

        Roscommon - Before July 26, 1858

    Relationship Status at Marriage - minor

Thomas Jones (father):

    Occupation - Gentleman

Christopher Knight (father):

    Occupation - Gentleman

Wedding Witnesses:

James Knight & Henry Knight

Signatures:

Hurst

- Clifford Knight & Mary Blackburne (B l a c k b u r n e) – 9 Dec 1672 (Marriage, **St. Peter Parish**)

- Daniel Knight & Catherine Knight

  o Margaret Knight & Michael Donnelly – 2 Feb 1861 (Marriage, **Chapelizod Parish (RC)**)

    ▪ Mary Maria Donnelly – b. 1862, bapt. 1862 (Baptism, **Chapelizod Parish (RC)**)

    ▪ James Donnelly – b. 1864, bapt. 1864 (Baptism, **Chapelizod Parish (RC)**)

Margaret Knight (daughter):

　Residence - Chapelizod - February 2, 1861

Michael Donnelly, son of James Donnelly (son-in-law):

　Residence - Blanchester - February 2, 1861

　　　Chapelizod - 1862

　　　　1864

- Daniel Knight & Margaret Knight

  o Margaret Knight – bapt. 16 Oct 1747 (Baptism, **Dingle Parish**)

Daniel Knight (father):

　Occupation - Soldier - October 16, 1747

- Daniel Knight & Mary Quirk

  o Anne Knight – bapt. 4 Mar 1815 (Baptism, **Bandon Parish (RC)**)

- Darby Knight & Mary Downey

  o Dennis Knight – bapt. 12 Feb 1808 (Baptism, **Bantry Parish (RC)**)

- Edmund Knight & Mary Mullarky – 8 Mar 1750 (Marriage, **St. Audoen Parish**) (Marriage, **St. Audoen Parish (RC)**)

- Edward Knight & Anne Ellis – 14 Nov 1758 (Marriage, **St. Audoen Parish**)

Knight Surname Ireland: 1600s to 1900s

- Edward Knight & Bridget McEvoy

  o Hannah Knight – b. 6 Aug 1868, bapt. 10 Aug 1868 (Baptism, **SS. Michael & John Parish (RC)**)

  o Bridget Knight – b. 1 Apr 1873, bapt. 7 Apr 1873 (Baptism, **SS. Michael & John Parish (RC)**)

Edward Knight (father):

Residence - 15 Wood Quay - August 10, 1868

April 7, 1873

- Edward Knight & Elizabeth Kinsella

  o Michael Knight – b. 30 Sep 1866, bapt. 10 Oct 1866 (Baptism, **St. Michan Parish (RC)**)

Edward Knight (father):

Residence - 4 Lisburn Street - October 10, 1866

- Edward Knight & Honora Knight

  o James Knight – bapt. 12 Jul 1744 (Baptism, **St. Catherine Parish (RC)**)

- Edward Knight & Jane Knight

  o Jane Knight – bapt. 17 Sep 1674 (Baptism, **St. Michan Parish**)

- Edward Knight & Joyce Knight

  o William Knight – bapt. 18 Feb 1663 (Baptism, **St. Michan Parish**)

- Edward Knight & Margaret Unknown

  o Mary Knight – bapt. 1747 (Baptism, **St. Andrew Parish (RC)**)

- Francis Knight & Elizabeth Knight, bur. 27 Apr 1698 (Burial, **St. Audoen Parish**)

- Francis Knight & Emma Knight

  o William James Knight – b. 12 Jun 1882, bapt. 9 Aug 1882 (Baptism, **Portobello Barracks Parish**)

Hurst

- Charles Stanley Knight – b. 12 Dec 1885, bapt. 17 Jan 1886 (Baptism, **Pigeon House Fort Parish**)

- Elizabeth Minnie Knight – b. 12 Mar 1887, bapt. 10 Apr 1887 (Baptism, **Pigeon House Fort Parish**)

- Charlotte May Knight – b. 29 Dec 1888, bapt. 28 Jan 1889 (Baptism, **Irishtown Parish**) (Baptism, **Pigeon House Fort Parish**)

- Albert Victor Knight – b. 7 Jan 1891, bapt. 5 Feb 1891 (Baptism, **Pigeon House Fort Parish**)

Francis Knight (father):

Residence - Portobello Barracks - August 9, 1882

Pigeon House Fort - January 17, 1886

April 10, 1887

January 27, 1889

February 5, 1891

Occupation - Corporal Royal Horse Artillery - August 9, 1882

Corporal Coast Brigade Royal Artillery - January 17, 1886

April 10, 1887

January 28, 1889

February 5, 1891

- Frederick Knight & Mary Anne Knight

  - George Leonard Knight – b. 6 Aug 1900, bapt. 2 Sep 1900 (Baptism, **Arbour Hill Barracks Parish**)

Frederick Knight (father):

Residence - Marlboro Barracks - September 2, 1900

Occupation - Sergeant Trumpeter 21st Lancers - September 2, 1900

Knight Surname Ireland: 1600s to 1900s

- George Knight & Bridget Wall

  o Mary A. Knight & Thomas Wall – 30 Nov 1895 (Marriage, **St. Mary, Pro Cathedral Parish (RC)**)

    ▪ George Joseph Wall – b. 1899, bapt. 1899 (Baptism, **St. Andrew Parish (RC)**)

Mary A. Knight (daughter):

  Residence - 39 North Buckingham Street - November 30, 1895

Thomas Wall, son of Patrick Wall & Bella Barry (son-in-law):

  Residence - Limerick - November 30, 1895

  10 Luke Street - 1899

Patrick Wall (father):

  Residence - Fermoy - November 30, 1895

  o George Knight, b. 1 Jul 1873, bapt. 3 Jul 1873 (Baptism, **Kinsale Parish (RC)**) & Jane Cullen – 7 Aug 1898 (Marriage, **St. Mary, Pro Cathedral Parish (RC)**)

    ▪ George Knight – b. 13 Jun 1899, bapt. 21 Jun 1899 (Baptism, **St. Mary, Pro Cathedral Parish (RC)**)

George Knight (son):

  Residence - 4 Corn Exchange Place - August 7, 1898

  Rotunda - June 21, 1899

Jane Cullen, daughter of John Cullen & Elizabeth Dobbs (daughter-in-law):

  Residence - 9 Lower Gloucester Street - August 7, 1898

John Cullen (father):

  Residence - 9 Lower Gloucester Street - August 7, 1898

George Knight (father):

  Residence - Higher Street - July 3, 1873

  4 Corn Exchange Place - August 7, 1898

Hurst

- George Knight & Elizabeth Knight

  - George William Edgar Knight – b. 19 Jan 1889, bapt. 13 Mar 1889 (Baptism, **Arbour Hill**

    Barracks Parish)

George Knight (father):

Residence - Royal Infirmary - March 13, 1889

Occupation - Corporal Medical Staff Corps - March 13, 1889

- George Knight & Eleanor Unknown

  - Arthur Robert Knight – b. 9 Aug 1895, bapt. 25 Sep 1895 (Baptism, **St. Matthew Parish**)

George Knight (father):

Residence - Pigeon House Fort - September 25, 1895

Occupation - Sergeant Major R. E. - September 25, 1895

- George Knight & Mary Kavanagh

  - Mary Teresa Knight – b. 3 Jul 1888, bapt. 5 Jul 1888 (Baptism, **SS. Michael & John Parish**

    (RC))

George Knight (father):

Residence - 29 Parliament Street - July 5, 1888

- George Knight & Mary Knight

  - George Knight – b. 15 Mar 1900, bapt. 8 Apr 1900 (Baptism, **St. Matthias Parish**)

George Knight (father):

Residence - 26 Lower Leeson Street - April 8, 1900

Occupation - Coachman - April 8, 1900

- George Knight & Susan Unknown

  - George Harold Walter Knight – b. 15 Jun 1893, bapt. 6 Sep 1893 (Baptism, **St. Matthew**

    Parish)

George Knight (father):

Residence - 2 Vavasour Square - September 6, 1893

Occupation - Company Sergeant - September 6, 1893

Knight Surname Ireland: 1600s to 1900s

- George Knight & Unknown

    o   Robert Knight – bur. 7 Dec 1666 (Burial, **St. John Parish**)

    o   Alice Knight – bur. 2 Jan 1667 (Burial, **St. John Parish**)

    o   Sarah Knight – bur. 2 Sep 1668 (Burial, **St. John Parish**)

    o   Charles Knight – bapt. 7 Jan 1669 (Baptism, **St. John Parish**)

- George Knight & Unknown

    o   John Henry Knight & Nannie Martha Miller – 28 Aug 1880 (Marriage, **St. Paul Parish**)

    ▪ Ellen Elizabeth Knight – b. 7 Jul 1881, bapt. 14 Aug 1881 (Baptism, **Arbour Hill**

    Barracks Parish)

John Henry Knight (son):

   Residence - Royal Barracks - August 28, 1880

   August 14, 1881

   Occupation - Private Scots Greys - August 28, 1880

   Private in Royal Scots Greys - August 14, 1881

Nannie Martha Miller, daughter of William Miller (daughter-in-law):

   Residence - Montpelier Hill - August 28, 1880

William Miller (father):

   Occupation - Shoemaker

George Knight (father):

   Occupation - Glassmaker

- George Knight & Unknown

  o Thomas Knight & Mary Quinlan – 11 Jul 1881 (Marriage, **St. Peter Parish**)

Signature:

Signatures (Marriage):

- John Thomas Knight – b. 19 Dec 1883, bapt. 16 Jan 1884 (Baptism, **Rathmines Parish**

  (RC))

Thomas Knight (son):

Residence - Portobello Barracks - July 11, 1881

Harold's Cross - January 16, 1884

Occupation - Royal Horse Artillery - July 11, 1881

Mary Quinlan, daughter of John Quinlan (daughter-in-law):

Residence - 122 Rathgar Road - July 11, 1881

John Quinlan (father):

Occupation - Laborer

George Knight (father):

Occupation - Laborer

Knight Surname Ireland: 1600s to 1900s

- George Knight & Unknown

    o Frederick Knight & Elizabeth McManus – 29 Aug 1881 (Marriage, **St. Mary Parish**)

Signatures:

  - George Knight – bapt. 7 Dec 1883 (Baptism, **South Dublin Union Parish**)

Frederick Knight (son):

   Residence - Beggar Bush Barracks - August 29, 1881

   Occupation - Soldier 47th Regiment - August 29, 1881

Elizabeth McManus, daughter of Joseph McManus (daughter-in-law):

   Residence - 2 Abbey Street - August 29, 1881

Joseph McManus (father):

   Occupation - Cage Maker

George Knight (father):

   Occupation - Auctioneer

Wedding Witnesses:

Joseph McManus & Ellen McManus

Signatures:

- George Knight & Unknown

Signatures:

o Anna Georgina Knight & Collins Baughman Hubbard – 17 Jul 1890 (Marriage, **St. Anne Parish**)

Signatures:

Anna Georgina Knight (daughter):

Residence - *5 Holles Street - July 17, 1890*

Relationship Status at Marriage - minor

Collins Baughman Hubbard, son of Bela Hubbard (son-in-law):

Residence - Morrison's Hotel, Dawson Street - July 17, 1890

Occupation - Banker - July 17, 1890

Relationship Status at Marriage - divorced

Bela Hubbard (father):

Occupation - Esquire

George Knight (father):

Occupation - Solicitor

Wedding Witnesses:

George Knight & Nanny Knight

Signatures:

- o Michael Elliott Knight & Mary Clemina (C l e m i n a) Young – 3 Aug 1898 (Marriage, St.

  Anne Parish)

Signatures:

Michael Elliott Knight (son):

    Residence - Hibernian Hotel, Dawson Street - August 3, 1898

            Clones, Co. Monaghan - August 3, 1898

    Occupation - Solicitor - August 3, 1898

Mary Clemina Young, daughter of Walter William Young (daughter-in-law):

    Residence - 19 Prince Patrick Terrace North Circular Road - August 3, 1898

    Relationship Status at Marriage - minor

Walter William Young (father):

    Occupation - Gentleman

George Knight (father):

    Occupation - Clerk of the Crown & Place, Co. Meath

Wedding Witnesses:

M. Glover, George Knight, & L. H. Knight

Signatures:

- Mary Geraldine Knight & Samuel Henry Bolton – 3 Jan 1900 (Marriage, **St. Matthias Parish**)

Signatures:

Knight Surname Ireland: 1600s to 1900s

Mary Geraldine Knight (daughter):

Residence - Lackanart Trim - January 3, 1900

Samuel Henry Bolton, son of Samuel Henry Bolton (son-in-law):

Residence - Grove House, Rathmines - January 3, 1900

Occupation - Civil Engineer - January 3, 1900

Samuel Henry Bolton (father):

Residence - Builder

George Knight (father):

Occupation - Clerk of Crown & Peace

Wedding Witnesses:

R. Denne Bolton & George Knight

Signatures:

Hurst

- George Knight & Unknown

    o George Knight & Mary Anne Coates – 22 Feb 1898 (Marriage, **St. Stephen Parish**)

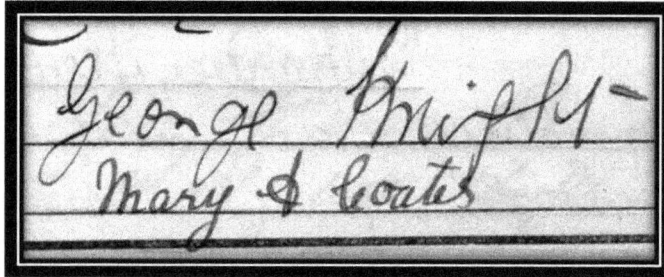

Signatures:

- Mary Knight – b. 1898, bapt. 1898 (Baptism, **Chapelizod Parish (RC)**)

- William George Knight – b. 15 Mar 1900, bapt. 7 Apr 1900 (Baptism, **Rathmines Parish (RC)**)

- Margaret Knight – b. 26 Nov 1901, bapt. 20 Dec 1901 (Baptism, **Harrington Street Parish (RC)**)

George Knight (son):

Residence - 44 Wellington Road - February 22, 1898

Knockmaroon - 1898

26 Lower Leeson Street - April 7, 1900

26 Hatch Lane - December 20, 1901

Occupation - Coachman - February 22, 1898

Mary Anne Coates, daughter of Thomas Coates (daughter-in-law):

Residence - 31A Holles Street - February 22, 1898

Thomas Coates (father):

Occupation - Carman

George Knight (father):

Occupation - Coachman

Knight Surname Ireland: 1600s to 1900s

- George Joseph Charles Knight & Mary Anne Knight

  - Nellie May Knight – b. 2 Feb 1893, bapt. 29 Mar 1893 (Baptism, **Ballyheigue Parish**)

    (Baptism, **Tralee Parish**), bur. 4 May 1896 (Burial, **Ballyheigue Parish**)

Nellie May Knight (daughter):

  Residence - Coast Guard Station, Ballyheigue - Before May 4, 1896

  Age at Death - 3 years

  - Winifred Knight – b. 4 Mar 1896, bapt. 6 Aug 1896 (Baptism, **Ballyheigue Parish**)

    (Baptism, **Tralee Parish**)

George Joseph Charles Knight (father):

  Residence - Coast Guard Station, Ballyheigue, Co. Kerry - March 29, 1893

                                            August 6, 1896

  Occupation - Coast Guard - March 29, 1893

                              August 6, 1896

- Gulielmo Knight & Mary Unknown

  - Henry Knight & Elizabeth Maguire – 28 Oct 1893 (Marriage, **St. Mary, Haddington Road**

    Parish (RC))

    - John Thomas Knight – b. 17 Feb 1900, bapt. 25 Feb 1900 (Baptism, **St. Joseph Parish**

      (RC))

    - Henry Richard Knight – b. 31 Oct 1901, bapt. 3 Nov 1901 (Baptism, **St. Joseph Parish**

      (RC))

Henry Knight (son):

  Residence - Fermoy - October 28, 1893

              Wasdale Lodge, Terenure - February 25, 1900

                          November 3, 1901

Elizabeth Maguire, daughter of Patrick Maguire & Mary A. Unknown

(daughter-in-law):

  Residence - 26 Shelbourne Road - October 28, 1893

Hurst

Patrick Maguire (father):

> Residence - Co. Wicklow

Gulielmo Knight (father):

> Residence - Sussex

- Henry Knight & Alice Knight

  o Henrietta Knight – b. 3 Sep 1856, bapt. 21 Sep 1856 (Baptism, **St. Mark Parish**)

  o William Henry Knight – b. 2 May 1863, bapt. 3 Jun 1863 (Baptism, **St. Mary Parish**)

  o Mary Williams Knight – b. 27 Mar 1865, bapt. 26 Apr 1865 (Baptism, **St. Mary Parish**)

Henry Knight (father):

> Residence - 7 Brunswick Street - September 21, 1856
>
> 65 Blessington Street - June 3, 1863
>
> April 26, 1865
>
> Occupation - Law Clerk - September 21, 1856
>
> Law agent & Clerk - June 3, 1863
>
> Agent - April 26, 1865

- Henry Knight & Alice Knight

  o Margaret Jane Knight – b. 6 Jul 1858, bapt. 8 Aug 1858 (Baptism, **St. Peter Parish**)

Henry Knight (father):

> Residence - No 7 Gubstan Terrace Mount Pleasant - August 8, 1858
>
> Occupation - Gentleman - August 8, 1858

- Henry Knight & Alice Unknown

  o Christabella Kinosiuelc Knight – b. 3 Jun 1860, bapt. 18 Jul 1860 (Baptism, **St. Stephen Parish**)

Henry Knight (father):

> Residence - 4 Fosterew Haddington Road - July 18, 1860
>
> Occupation - Esquire - July 18, 1860

Knight Surname Ireland: 1600s to 1900s

- Henry Knight & Bridget Keeney – 27 Nov 1831 (Marriage, **St. Andrew Parish (RC)**)

- Henry Knight & Mary Barnes

  o Alexander Knight & Janet Hickie – 8 Sep 1881 (Marriage, **Ballylongford Parish (RC)**)

Alexander Knight (son):

Residence - Devonshire - September 8, 1881

Janet Hickie, daughter of George Hickie (daughter-in-law):

Residence - Kilelton - September 8, 1881

- Henry Knight & Mary Conner – 7 Oct 1839 (Marriage, **SS. Michael & John Parish (RC)**)

- Henry Knight & Mary Knight

  o Henry Knight & Helen Walsh – 21 Nov 1877 (Marriage, **Harrington Street Parish**

    (RC))

Henry Knight (son):

Residence - Axminster, Devon, England - November 21, 1877

Helen Walsh, daughter of Thomas Walsh & Mary Walsh (daughter-in-law):

Residence - 74 Harcourt Street - November 21, 1877

- Henry Knight & Sarah Unknown

  o William Henry Knight – b. 9 Jun 1884, bapt. 2 Jul 1884 (Baptism, **Tralee Parish**)

Henry Knight (father):

Residence - Tralee - July 2, 1884

Occupation - Private, 2ⁿᵈ Queen's Regiment - July 2, 1884

Hurst

- Henry Knight & Unknown

  o Henrietta Knight & John Gordon – 31 Mar 1884 (Marriage, St. Peter Parish)

Signatures:

Henrietta Knight (daughter):

    Residence - 6 Upper Rutland Street - March 31, 1884

John Gordon, son of Alexander Gordon (son-in-law):

    Residence - 35 Ranelagh Road - March 31, 1884

    Occupation - Chemist - March 31, 1884

Alexander Gordon (father):

Signature:

    Occupation - Chemist

Henry Knight (father):

    Occupation - Solicitor

Knight Surname Ireland: 1600s to 1900s

Wedding Witnesses:

Alexander Gordon & Alice Knight

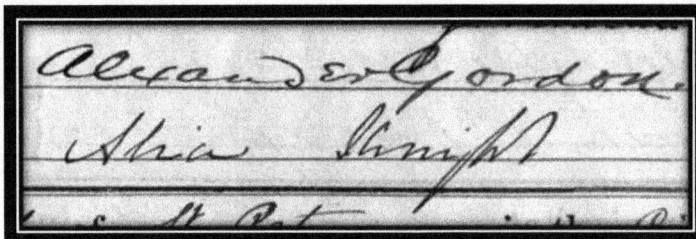

Signatures:

- Henry Knight & Unknown

  - William Henry Knight & Emily Louisa Moore – 4 May 1893 (Marriage, **Sandford Parish**)

    - Hilda Knight – b. 16 Aug 1894, bapt. 28 Oct 1894 (Baptism, **Rathmines Parish**)

    - William Henry Knight – b. 7 Mar 1896, bapt. 10 Jun 1896 (Baptism, **Rathmines Parish**)

    - Robert Knight – b. 27 Mar 1897, bapt. 30 May 1897 (Baptism, **Rathmines Parish**)

    - Reginald Knight – b. 25 Jan 1899, bapt. 16 Apr 1899 (Baptism, **Rathmines Parish**)

William Henry Knight (son):

Residence - 37 Frankfurt Avenue, Rathgar - May 4, 1893

37 Frankfurt Avenue - October 28, 1894

17 Annesley Park - June 10, 1896

May 30, 1897

April 16, 1899

Occupation - Railway Clerk - May 4, 1893

Clerk - October 28, 1894

June 10, 1896

May 30, 1897

April 16, 1899

Emily Louisa Moore, daughter of Robert Moore (daughter-in-law):

Residence - 8 Ashfield Road, Ranelagh - May 4, 1893

Robert Moore (father):

Occupation - Sub Agent

Hurst

Henry Knight (father):

Occupation - Land & Law Agent - May 4, 1893

Wedding Witnesses:

Henry Knight & Mary Constance Moore

- Henry Knight & Unknown

  o Walter George Knight & Emily Waldron – 22 Feb 1896 (Marriage, **St. Mary Parish**)

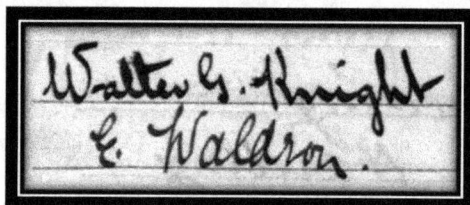

Signatures:

- Charles Bernard Knight – b. 12 Oct 1897, bapt. 31 Oct 1897 (Baptism, **St. George Parish**)

- Florence Emily Knight – b. 19 Apr 1899, bapt. 3 Sep 1899 (Baptism, **St. Barnabas Parish**)

- Edith Knight – bapt. 10 Nov 1900 (Baptism, **St. Barnabas Parish**)

Walter George Knight (son):

Residence - 20 Besboro Terrace, North Circular Road - February 22, 1896

20 Whitworth Road - October 31, 1897

11 Russell Avenue - September 3, 1899

November 10, 1900

Occupation - Canteen Steward - February 22, 1896

Journalist - October 31, 1897

Secretary Dublin Mineral Association - September 3, 1899

November 10, 1900

Emily Waldron, daughter of James Waldron (daughter-in-law):

Residence - 26 Rutland Street - February 22, 1896

Occupation - Dressmaker - February 22, 1896

Knight Surname Ireland: 1600s to 1900s

James Waldron (father):

    Occupation - Engine Driver

Henry Knight (father):

    Occupation - Army Pensioner

Wedding Witnesses:

Bernard H. Knight & Phoebe G. Knight

Signatures:

- Henry Ecklin Knight & Agnes Knight, bur. 30 Jun 1718 (Burial, **St. John Parish**)

- Henry Low Knight & Unknown

  o John Henry Knight & Emily Constance Hughes – 7 Jul 1883 (Marriage, **North Strand**

  Parish)

Signature:

Signatures (Marriage):

Hurst

John Henry Knight (son):

>   Residence - Island Bridge Barracks - July 7, 1883

>   Occupation - Clerk - July 7, 1883

Emily Constance Hughes, daughter of Richard Hughes (daughter-in-law):

>   Residence - 13 St. Brigids Avenue, North Strand - July 7, 1883

Richard Hughes (father):

>   Occupation - Woolen Draper

Henry Low Knight (father):

>   Occupation - Waiter

- Henry W. Knight & Elizabeth Leahy

    o   William Knight – b. 4 Aug 1873, bapt. 6 Aug 1873 (Baptism, Castleisland Parish (RC))

    o   Mary Knight – b. 23 Apr 1875, bapt. 25 Apr 1875 (Baptism, Castleisland Parish (RC))

    o   Samuel Knight – b. 1 Feb 1877, bapt. 4 Feb 1877 (Baptism, Castleisland Parish (RC))

    o   Elizabeth Knight – b. 10 Jun 1878, bapt. 16 Jun 1878 (Baptism, Castleisland Parish (RC))

    o   Honora Knight – b. 28 Jan 1881, bapt. 29 Jan 1881 (Baptism, Castleisland Parish (RC))

    o   Michael Knight – b. 1 Apr 1883, bapt. 14 Apr 1883 (Baptism, Castleisland Parish (RC))

    o   Ellen Knight – b. 6 Mar 1885, bapt. 7 Mar 1885 (Baptism, Castleisland Parish (RC))

    o   Henry Knight – b. 6 Jan 1887, bapt. 9 Jan 1887 (Baptism, Castleisland Parish (RC))

    o   Margaret Knight – b. 27 Nov 1896, bapt. 1 Dec 1896 (Baptism, Castleisland Parish (RC))

Knight Surname Ireland: 1600s to 1900s

Henry Knight (father):

Residence - Castleisland - August 6, 1873

February 4, 1877

Millview - April 25, 1875

Kielegane - June 16, 1878

January 29, 1881

March 7, 1885

January 9, 1887

Dulague - April 14, 1883

Hillview - December 1, 1896

- Hugo Knight & Anne Phelan – 18 Jun 1811 (Marriage, **St. Andrew Parish (RC)**)

  o Gulielmo Knight – bapt. 1813 (Baptism, **St. Andrew Parish (RC)**)

  o Eleanor Knight – bapt. 1815 (Baptism, **St. Andrew Parish (RC)**)

- Hugo Knight & Mary Miller

  o Hugo Knight – b. 20 Jan 1879, bapt. 24 Jan 1879 (Baptism, **Harrington Street Parish**

  (RC))

Hugo Knight (father):

Residence - 10 New Street - January 24, 1879

- Humphrey Knight & Anne Unknown

  o James Knight – bapt. 28 Apr 1738 (Baptism, **St. John Parish**)

- Humphrey Knight & Elizabeth Carter – 29 Dec 1693 (Marriage, **St. Andrew Parish**)

- Humphrey Knight & Margaret Knight'

  o James Knight – bapt. 4 May 1727 (Baptism, **St. Catherine Parish**)

- Humphrey Knight & Margaret Unknown

  o Isabel Knight – bapt. 20 Jun 1741 (Baptism, **St. John Parish**)

  o George Knight – bapt. 6 Feb 1742 (Baptism, **St. John Parish**)

Hurst

- Humphrey Knight & Mary Unknown

  - Mary Knight – bapt. 25 Jun 1735 (Baptism, **St. John Parish**)

- Isaac Knight & Elizabeth Cole

  - Sarah Knight – bapt. 3 Jan 1820 (Baptism, **Bandon Parish (RC)**)

- Isaac Knight, bur. 23 Jun 1785 (Burial, **St. Luke Parish**) & Elizabeth Knight

  - Alice Knight – bur. 31 Dec 1780 (Burial, **St. Luke Parish**)

Alice Knight (daughter):

Cause of Death - small pox

  - Burton Knight – bapt. 20 Sep 1778 (Baptism, **St. Luke Parish**), bur. 20 Mar 1781 (Burial, **St. Luke Parish**)

Burton Knight (son):

Cause of Death - jaundice

Isaac Knight (father):

Residence - New Market - September 20, 1778

Brabazon Row - December 31, 1780

March 20, 1781

New Row - June 23, 1785

Occupation - Hosier - September 20, 1778

Cause of Death - fever

- James Knight & Elizabeth Knight

  - William Knight – bapt. 17 Aug 1696 (Baptism, **St. Michan Parish**), bur. 13 Nov 1697 (Burial, **St. Michan Parish**)

  - Charles Knight – bur. 16 Nov 1698 (Burial, **St. Michan Parish**)

  - Charles Knight – bapt. 8 May 1702 (Baptism, **St. Mary Parish**)

  - Anne Knight – bapt. 24 Apr 1704 (Baptism, **St. Mary Parish**), bur 12 Nov 1705 (Burial, **St. Mary Parish**)

Knight Surname Ireland: 1600s to 1900s

- o John Knight – bur. 7 Sep 1704 (Burial, **St. Mary Parish**)

James Knight (father):

Occupation - Glasier - August 17, 1696

November 13, 1697

November 16, 1698

May 8, 1702

April 24, 1704

September 7, 1704

November 12, 1705

- James Knight & Georgina Lynch

  - o James Knight – bapt. 13 Oct 1845 (Baptism, **Kilmacabea Parish (RC)**)

- James Knight & Jane Knight, bur. 3 Sep 1699 (Burial, **St. Michan Parish**)

Jane Knight (wife):

Occupation - Begger - Before September 3, 1699

- James Knight & Jane Lynch – 14 Aug 1819 (Marriage, **Cork - South Parish (RC)**)

  - o Jane Knight – bapt. 22 Mar 1825 (Baptism, **Cork - South Parish (RC)**)

  - o James Knight – bapt. 21 May 1828 (Baptism, **Cork - South Parish (RC)**)

Jane Lynch (mother):

Residence - Vicar Street - August 14, 1819

- James Knight & Margaret Knight

  - o Anne Knight – bapt. 6 Mar 1747 (Baptism, **Dingle Parish**)

- James Knight & Mary Moncall – 14 Jun 1758 (Marriage, **St. Anne Parish**)

James Knight (husband):

Professional Title - Reverend Dr.

Mary Moncall (wife):

Relationship Status at Marriage -widow

Hurst

- James Knight & Mary Murphy

  o Mary Knight – b. 15 Apr 1856, bapt. 29 Sep 1856 (Baptism, *St. Mary, Pro Cathedral Parish (RC)*)

James Knight (father):

Residence - 5 Mecklenburgh Street - September 29, 1856

- James Knight & Unknown

  o Elizabeth Knight – bapt. 13 Feb 1643 (Baptism, *St. John Parish*), bur. 28 Apr 1644 (Burial, *St. John Parish*)

- James Knight & Unknown

  o William Knight – bur. 18 Oct 1691 (Burial, *St. John Parish*)

- James Ellis Knight & Julia Clare Riordan – 13 Aug 1805 (Marriage, *Cork - South Parish (RC)*)

  o Julia Knight – bapt. 1 Nov 1809 (Baptism, *Cork - South Parish (RC)*)

James Ellis Knight (father):

Residence - Dyke - November 1, 1809

Julia Clare Riordan (mother):

Residence - Anne Street - August 13, 1805

- James Irwin Knight & Unknown

  o Alexander Knight & Jane Cochrane Brady – 1 Apr 1863 (Marriage, *St. Peter Parish*)

Signatures:

Knight Surname Ireland: 1600s to 1900s

Alexander Knight (son):

    Residence - Cloney Parish - April 1, 1863

    Occupation - M. D. - April 1, 1863

Jane Cochrane Brady, daughter of John Brady (daughter-in-law):

    Residence - 5 Camden Street - April 1, 1863

John Brady (father):

    Occupation - Banker

James Irwin Knight (father):

    Occupation - Solicitor

Wedding Witnesses:

William Moore & John Cochrane Brady

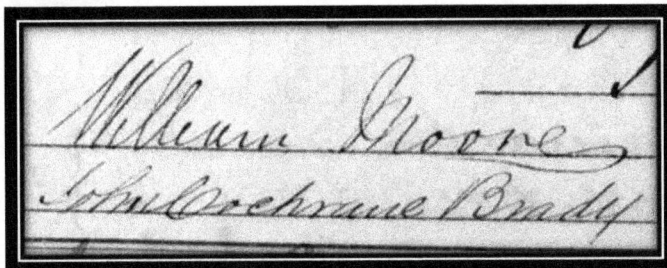

Signatures:

- John Knight & Anne Carey

  - John Knight – bapt. 7 Jan 1801 (Baptism, **Cork - South Parish (RC)**)

John Knight (father):

    Residence - Dunbar Street - January 7, 1801

- John Knight & Anne Cleary

  - Elizabeth Knight – bapt. 25 Mar 1799 (Baptism, **Cork - South Parish (RC)**)

  - David Knight – bapt. 29 May 1803 (Baptism, **Cork - SS. Peter & Paul Parish (RC)**)

Hurst

- John Knight & Anne Hoey

  o Mary Knight & John Carey – 22 Oct 1879 (Marriage, **St. Mary, Pro Cathedral Parish (RC)**)

Mary Knight (daughter):

Residence - 45 Marlboro Street - October 22, 1879

John Carey, son of John Carey & Bridget Green (son-in-law):

Residence - 54 Marlboro Street - October 22, 1879

John Carey (father):

Residence - Co. Longford - October 22, 1879

John Knight (father):

Residence - Rusk - October 22, 1879

- John Knight & Anne Knight

  o Charles Knight – bapt. 12 Sep 1747 (Baptism, **Dingle Parish**)

John Knight (father):

Occupation - Soldier - September 12, 1747

- John Knight & Bridget Smith – 11 Oct 1841 (Marriage, **St. Andrew Parish (RC)**)

  o Mary Knight – bapt. 12 Jan 1843 (Baptism, **St. James Parish (RC)**)

- John Knight & Catherine Austin

  o Joseph Knight – b. 23 Apr 1867, bapt. 6 May 1867 (Baptism, **St. Mary, Pro Cathedral Parish (RC)**)

John Knight (father):

Residence - 6 Temple Street - May 6, 1867

Knight Surname Ireland: 1600s to 1900s

- John Knight, bur. 21 Feb 1696 (Burial, **St. Michan Parish**) & Catherine Knight

    o   Mary Knight – bapt. 20 Oct 1664 (Baptism, **St. Michan Parish**)

    o   Sarah Knight – bapt. 29 May 1666 (Baptism, **St. Michan Parish**)

    o   Richard Knight – bapt. 4 Sep 1670 (Baptism, **St. Michan Parish**)

    o   Anne Knight – bur. 30 Nov 1686 (Burial, **St. Michan Parish**)

John Knight (father):

Occupation - Poulterer - September 4, 1670

November 30, 1686

Before February 21, 1696

- John Knight & Catherine Leary

    o   Joseph Knight – b. 26 Jul 1823, bapt. 26 Jul 1826 (Baptism, **Castletownbere Parish (RC)**)

John Knight (father):

Residence - Ririn - July 26, 1826

- John Knight & Dorothy Knight

    o   Jane Knight – bapt. 16 Apr 1674 (Baptism, **St. Michan Parish**)

John Knight (father):

Occupation - Gentleman - April 16, 1674

- John Knight & Eleanor Knight

    o   John Knight – bur. 26 Jun 1710 (Burial, **St. Audoen Parish**)

- John Knight & Elizabeth Campbell – 23 Dec 1756 (Marriage, **St. Luke Parish**)

- John Knight & Elizabeth Knight

    o   Elizabeth Knight – bapt. 5 Dec 1862 (Baptism, **St. Audoen Parish**)

- John Knight & Elizabeth Unknown

    o   Anne Knight – bapt. 1849 (Baptism, **St. Mary, Haddington Road Parish (RC)**)

Hurst

- John Knight & Ellen Mahoney

  - Jonathan Knight – bapt. 23 Sep 1820 (Baptism, **Kilbrittain Parish** (RC))

  - James Knight – Sep 1823 (Baptism, **Kilbrittain Parish** (RC))

  - Jonathan Knight – bapt. 23 Nov 1828 (Baptism, **Kilbrittain Parish** (RC))

  - Patrick Knight – bapt. 22 May 1826 (Baptism, **Kilbrittain Parish** (RC))

  - Mary Knight – bapt. 28 Nov 1831 (Baptism, **Kilbrittain Parish** (RC))

- John Knight & Esther Knight

  - William Knight – bapt. 26 Nov 1827 (Baptism, **St. Mary, Pro Cathedral Parish** (RC))

John Knight (father):

Residence - Clarendon Street - November 26, 1827

- John Knight & Honora Murhill – 22 Aug 1848 (Marriage, **Killarney Parish** (RC))

  - Mary Knight – b. 30 Mar 1851, bapt. 30 Mar 1851 (Baptism, **Killarney Parish** (RC))

  - Margaret Knight – b. 19 Dec 1852, bapt. 19 Dec 1852 (Baptism, **Killarney Parish** (RC))

  - Catherine Knight – b. 1 Oct 1854, bapt. 1 Oct 1854 (Baptism, **Killarney Parish** (RC))

  - Honora Knight – b. 28 Sep 1856, bapt. 28 Sep 1856 (Baptism, **Killarney Parish** (RC))

  - Michael Knight – b. 3 Dec 1860, bapt. 4 Dec 1860 (Baptism, **Killarney Parish** (RC))

John Knight (father):

Residence - Killarney - August 22, 1848

March 30, 1851

December 19, 1852

October 1, 1854

December 28, 1856

December 4, 1860

Honora Murhill (mother):

Residence - Killarney - August 22, 1848

Knight Surname Ireland: 1600s to 1900s

- John Knight & Honora Sweeney – 28 Nov 1818 (Marriage, **Kilbrittain & Rathclareen Parish (RC)**)

  o Mary Knight – bapt. 3 Sep 1819 (Baptism, **Kilbrittain Parish (RC)**)

  o Anne Knight – bapt. 15 Mar 1822 (Baptism, **Kilbrittain Parish (RC)**)

  o John Knight – bapt, 12 Mar 1825 (Baptism, **Courcy's Country or Ballinspittal Parish (RC)**)

  o Elizabeth Knight – bapt. 21 Feb 1829 (Baptism, **Courcy's Country or Ballinspittal Parish (RC)**)

  o Joan Knight – bapt. 1 Jan 1831 (Baptism, **Courcy's Country or Ballinspittal Parish (RC)**)

  o James Knight – bapt. 14 Feb 1834 (Baptism, **Courcy's Country or Ballinspittal Parish (RC)**)

- John Knight & Jane Cavanagh

  o Mary Jane Knight – b. 23 Nov 1890, bapt. 23 Nov 1890 (Baptism, **Listowel Parish (RC)**)

  o Susan Knight – b. 23 Nov 1890, bapt. 23 Nov 1890 (Baptism, **Listowel Parish (RC)**)

John Knight (father):

Residence - Listowel - November 23, 1890

- John Knight & Jane Unknown

  o Catherine Knight – b. 26 Dec 1862, bapt. 28 Dec 1862 (Baptism, **Rathmines Parish (RC)**)

John Knight (father):

Residence - Rathmines - December 28, 1862

- John Knight & Joan Connolly

  o Ellen Knight – bapt. 8 Feb 1835 (Baptism, **Bantry Parish (RC)**)

Hurst

- John Knight & Joan Sweeney

  o Catherine Knight – bapt. Dec 1826 (Baptism, **Courcy's Country or Ballinspittal Parish (RC)**)

- John Knight & Lydia Knight

  o John Knight – bapt. 25 Feb 1759 (Baptism, **St. Audoen Parish**)

  o William Knight – bapt. 23 Nov 1760 (Baptism, **St. Audoen Parish**)

- John Knight & Margaret Byrne (B y r n e)

  o John Knight – bapt. Sep 1851 (Baptism, **St. Michan Parish (RC)**)

- John Knight & Margaret Knight

  o Simon Knight – bapt. 1829 (Baptism, **Palmerstown Parish (RC)**)

  o Mary Anne Knight – bapt. 1832 (Baptism, **Palmerstown Parish (RC)**)

- John Knight & Martha Knight

  o John Knight – b. 17 Feb 1841, bapt. 28 May 1841 (Baptism, **St. Mark Parish**)

John Knight (father):
Residence - City Quay - May 28, 1841
Occupation - Sailor - May 28, 1841

- John Knight & Mary Gordon – Unclear (Marriage, **St. Peter Parish**)

- John Knight & Mary Knight

  o Philip Knight – bapt. 14 Apr 1712 (Baptism, **St. Catherine Parish**)

- John Knight & Mary Knight

  o Sarah Knight – bapt. 3 Jun 1722 (Baptism, **St. Paul Parish**)

- John Knight & Mary Knight

  o James Knight – bapt. 8 Jun 1800 (Baptism, **St. Mary Parish**)

Knight Surname Ireland: 1600s to 1900s

- John Knight & Maud Elizabeth Helena Knight

  o Lily Maud Knight – b. 5 May 1898, bapt. 29 May 1898 (Baptism, **Arbour Hill Barracks Parish**)

John Knight (father):

Residence -33 Montpelier Hill - May 29, 1898

Occupation - Warder - May 29, 1898

- John Knight & Phyllis Knight

  o James Knight – bapt. 22 Aug 1770 (Baptism, **St. Audoen Parish**)

  o Joseph Knight – bapt. 6 Jul 1773 (Baptism, **St. Luke Parish**)

John Knight (father):

Residence - Corn Market - July 6, 1773

Occupation - Hosier - July 6, 1773

- John Knight & Rebecca Knight

  o Heneryeus Marya Knight (daughter) – b. 18 Feb 1716, bapt. 26 Feb 1716 (Baptism, **St. John Parish**), bur. 15 Mar 1716 (Burial, **St. John Parish**)

John Knight (father):

Residence - Blind Key - February 26, 1716

Occupation - Gentleman - February 26, 1716

- John Knight & Sarah Carty

  o Francis Knight – bapt. 21 Jun 1787 (Baptism, **St. Michan Parish (RC)**)

  o Sarah Knight – bapt. 21 Jun 1787 (Baptism, **St. Michan Parish (RC)**)

- John Knight & Sarah Knight

  o Phyllis Knight – bapt. 18 Apr 1708 (Baptism, **St. Catherine Parish**)

- John Knight & Sarah Knight

  o Stephen Knight – bapt. 27 Apr 1730 (Baptism, **St. Luke Parish**)

  o Anne Knight – bapt. 9 Jul 1732 (Baptism, **St. Luke Parish**)

Hurst

- John Knight & Sarah Knight

  - George Knight – bapt. 11 Jan 1778 (Baptism, **St. Mary Parish**)

- John Knight & Sarah Unknown

  - Martin Knight – bapt. 16 Oct 1698 (Baptism, **St. Catherine Parish**)

- John Knight & Sarah Unknown

  - Elizabeth Knight – bapt. 2 May 1785 (Baptism, **St. Mary, Pro Cathedral Parish (RC)**)

- John Knight & Susan Knight

  - Gulielmo Alfred Knight & Elizabeth Brien – 27 Apr 1867 (Marriage, **St. Mary, Pro Cathedral Parish (RC)**)

Gulielmo Alfred Knight (son):

  Residence - 114 Summer Hill - April 27, 1867

Elizabeth Brien, daughter of James Brien & Mary Brien (daughter-in-law):

  Residence - 29 Summer Hill - April 27, 1867

James Brien (father):

  Residence - Kilkeffare

John Knight (father):

  Residence - Manchester

- John Knight & Unknown

  - Elizabeth Knight – bapt. 7 Feb 1635 (Baptism, **St. John Parish**)

  - Margaret Knight – bapt. 30 Apr 1637 (Baptism, **St. John Parish**)

  - Susanna Knight – bapt. 7 Apr 1639 (Baptism, **St. John Parish**)

- John Knight & Unknown

  - Margaret Knight – bapt. 19 Aug 1657 (Baptism, **St. John Parish**)

- John Knight & Unknown

  - Sarah Knight – bur. 30 Jul 1678 (Burial, **St. Nicholas Within Parish**)

Knight Surname Ireland: 1600s to 1900s

- John Knight & Unknown

  o John Knight – bapt. 9 Nov 1697 (Baptism, **St. Catherine Parish**)

- John Knight & Unknown

  o Margaret Knight – bapt. 16 Dec 1700 (Baptism, **St. Peter Parish**)

John Knight (father):

Residence - Kevin Street - December 16, 1700

- John Knight & Unknown

  o Ellen Knight & Edward Bulger – 10 Nov 1845 (Marriage, **St. Catherine Parish**)

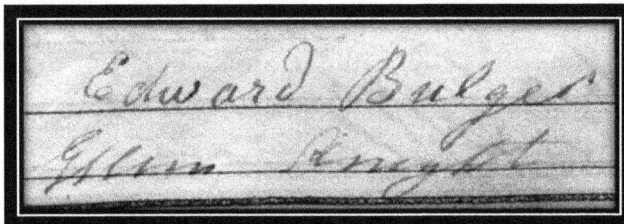

Signatures:

Ellen Knight (daughter):

Residence - Thomas Street - November 10, 1845

Edward Bulger, son of Edward Bulger (son-in-law):

Residence - Thomas Street - November 10, 1845

Occupation - Brazier - November 10, 1845

Edward Bulger (father):

Occupation - Brazier

John Knight (father):

Occupation - Farmer

- John Knight & Unknown

  o George Knight & Hannah McAllister – 31 Aug 1851 (Marriage, **St. Audoen Parish**)

Signatures:

George Knight (son):

    Residence - Royal Barracks - August 31, 1851

    Occupation - Soldier - August 31, 1851

Hannah McAllister, daughter of Randal McAllister (daughter-in-law):

    Residence - 7 Silver Street - August 31, 1851

Randal McAllister (father):

    Occupation - Foundry Man

John Knight (father):

    Occupation - Gardiner

Knight Surname Ireland: 1600s to 1900s

- John Knight & Unknown

  - Margaret Knight & Robert McMullen – 6 Apr 1858 (Marriage, **St. Werburgh Parish**)

Signatures:

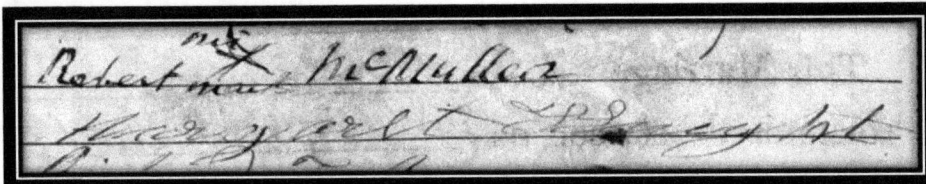

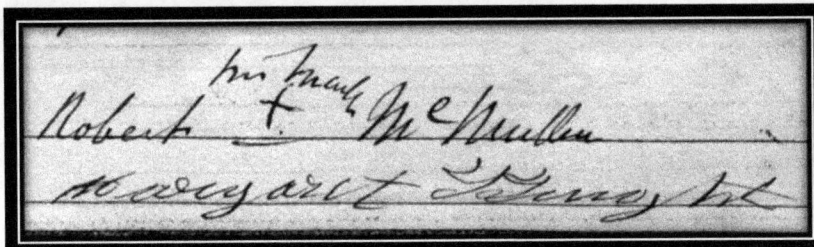

Margaret Knight (daughter):

    Residence - 42 Essex Street - April 6, 1858

Robert McMullen, son of William McMullen (son-in-law):

    Residence - 42 Essex Street - April 6, 1858

    Occupation - Van Coachman - April 6, 1858

    Relationship Status at Marriage - widow

William McMullen (father):

    Occupation - Weaver

John Knight (father):

    Occupation - Sailor

Hurst

- John Knight & Unknown

  - William Alfred Knight & Elizabeth Bryan – 27 Apr 1867 (Marriage, **St. Mark Parish**)

Signatures:

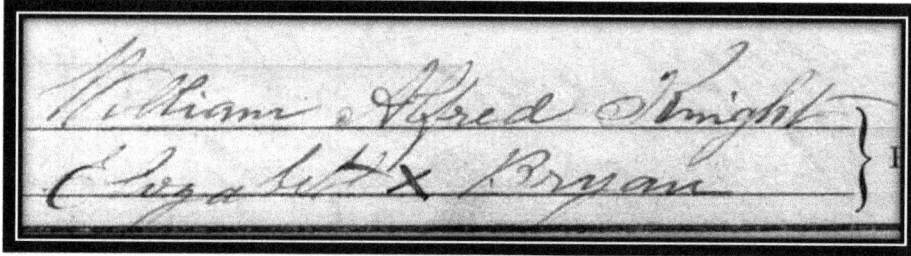

William Alfred Knight (son):

    Residence - 80 Brunswick Street - April 27, 1867

    Occupation - Commercial Traveller - April 27, 1867

Elizabeth Bryan, daughter of James Bryan (daughter-in-law):

    Residence - 80 Brunswick Street - April 27, 1867

James Bryan (father):

    Occupation - Farmer

John Knight (father):

    Occupation - Cotton Manufacturer

- John Knight & Unknown

  - Emily Knight & George Bradlaugh – 26 May 1870 (Marriage, **Taney Parish**)

Emily Knight (daughter):

    Residence - Taney Hill - May 26, 1870

    Occupation - Servant - May 26, 1870

Gorge Bradlaugh, son of James Bradlaugh (son-in-law):

    Residence - Taney Hill - May 26, 1870

    Occupation - Servant - May 26, 1870

Knight Surname Ireland: 1600s to 1900s

James Bradlaugh (father):

    Occupation - Servant

John Knight (father):

    Occupation - Tradesman

- John Knight & Unknown

      o   Henry Knight & Anne Middleton – 23 Jan 1871 (Marriage, **St. Mary Parish**)

Signatures:

Henry Knight (son):

    Residence - 32 Upper Dorset Street - January 23, 1871

    Occupation - Mariner - January 23, 1871

Anne Middleton, daughter of William Middleton (daughter-in-law):

    Residence - 2 Charlemont Terrace, Kingstown - January 23, 1871

William Middleton (father):

    Occupation - Railway Overseer

John Knight (father):

    Occupation - Mariner

Wedding Witnesses:

John Wilson & Daniel Knight

Signatures:

Hurst

- John Knight & Unknown

  - James Edward Knight & Anne Beach – 4 Nov 1893 (Marriage, **St. Werburgh Parish**)

    - John William Knight – b. 1898, bapt. 1899 (Baptism, **St. Thomas Parish**)

Signatures:

James Edward Knight (son):

    Residence - 48 South Great George's Street - November 4, 1893

        6 & 7 Colis Lane, Dublin - 1899

    Occupation - Show Proprietor - November 4, 1893

        [Commercial] Traveller - 1899

Anne Beach, daughter of John Beach (daughter-in-law):

    Residence - 8 Woodbridge Cottages, Turnham Green - November 4, 1893

John Beach (father):

    Occupation - Show Proprietor

John Knight (father):

    Occupation - Banker

Knight Surname Ireland: 1600s to 1900s

- John Knight & Unknown

  o John Knight, b. 1876, & Mary Ellen Peyton – 4 Jan 1899 (Marriage, **North Strand Parish**)

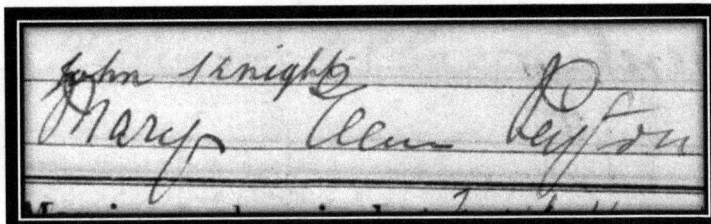

Signatures:

John Knight (son):

Residence - R M S "Leinster" Kingstown - January 4, 1899

Occupation - Cook - January 4, 1899

Age at Marriage - 23 years

Mary Ellen Peyton, daughter of James Peyton (daughter-in-law):

Residence - 62 Ballybaugh Road - January 4, 1899

James Peyton (father):

Occupation - Gas Inspector

John Knight (father):

Occupation - Sailor

- John Dillon Knight & Grace Knight

  o Elizabeth Knight – bapt. 27 Sep 1703 (Baptism, **St. Paul Parish**)

  o Thomas Knight – bapt. 4 Aug 1704 (Baptism, **St. Paul Parish**)

- John W. Knight & Unknown

  - Arthur Corscadden Knight & Frances Flower – 28 Aug 1895 (Marriage, **Leeson Park Parish**)

Signatures:

Arthur Corscadden Knight (son):

    Residence - 2 Chelmsford Road, Ranelagh, Dublin - August 28, 1895

        Portsmouth - August 28, 1895

    Occupation - Sergeant Royal Artillery - August 28, 1895

Frances Flower, daughter of Isaac Flower (daughter-in-law):

    Residence - 1 Eccles Street, Dublin - August 28, 1895

        Portsmouth - August 28, 1895

Isaac Flower (father):

    Occupation - Farmer

John W. Knight (father):

    Occupation - School Master

Wedding Witnesses:

Frederick Robert Flower & Amelia C. Knight

Signatures:

Knight Surname Ireland: 1600s to 1900s

- Jonah Knight & Margaret Houlihan

  o Cornelius (C o r n e l i u s) Knight – bapt. 18 Sep 1791 (Baptism, **Bantry Parish (RC)**)

- Jonathan Knight & Julia Sweeney – Feb 1824 (Marriage, **Kilbrittain & Rathclareen Parish (RC)**)

  o Anne Knight – bapt. 3 Aug 1828 (Baptism, **Courcy's Country or Ballinspittal Parish (RC)**)

- Joseph Knight & Elizabeth Daly – 28 Apr 1794 (Marriage, **Cork - South Parish (RC)**)

- Joseph Knight & Mary Anne Knight, b. Sep 1842, d. 21 Nov 1869, bur. 22 Nov 1869 (Burial, **Arbour Hill Barracks Parish**)

  o Lily Jane Knight – b. 8 Nov 1869, bapt. 20 Nov 1869 (Baptism, **Arbour Hill Barracks Parish**), d. 22 Nov 1869, bur. 23 Nov 1869 (Burial, **Arbour Hill Barracks Parish**)

Lily Jane Knight (daughter):
> **Residence - Richmond Barracks - November 22, 1869**
> **Age at Death - 12 days**

Joseph Knight (father):
> **Residence - Richmond Barracks - November 20, 1869**
> **Occupation - Color Sergeant 1/17th - November 20, 1869**

Mary Anne Knight (mother):
> **Residence - Richmond Barracks - November 22, 1869**

- Joseph Knight & Sarah Quinn – 14 Aug 1796 (Marriage, **St. Andrew Parish (RC)**)

Hurst

- Joshua George Knight & Unknown

  o John George Knight & Anastasia Hanrick (H a n r i c k) – 12 Jun 1882 (Marriage, **St. George Parish**)

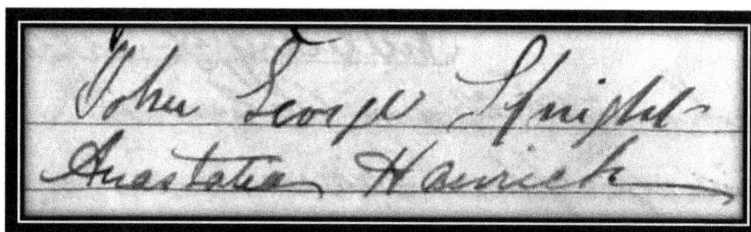

Signatures:

- Jemima Mary Knight – b. 11 Oct 1883, bapt. 19 Oct 1883 (Baptism, **St. Michan Parish (RC)**)

- John Harold Knight – b. 12 Jan 1885, bapt. 2 Feb 1885 (Baptism, **St. Michan Parish (RC)**)

- Isabel Patricia Florence Knight – b. 14 Mar 1887, bapt. 6 Apr 1887 (Baptism, **Rathmines Parish (RC)**)

- Mabel Dorothea Mary Knight – b. 9 Aug 1888, bapt. 5 Sep 1888 (Baptism, **Rathmines Parish (RC)**)

- Georgina Alice Maud Knight – b. 2 Aug 1891, bapt. 26 Aug 1891 (Baptism, **Rathmines Parish (RC)**)

John George Knight (son):

Residence - 5 Doyle Road, Drumcondra - June 12, 1882

October 19, 1883

February 2, 1885

Lower Mount Pleasant Avenue - April 6, 1887

Mount Pleasant Square - September 5, 1888

15 Upper Beechwood Avenue, Ranelagh - August 26, 1891

Occupation - Watch Maker - June 19, 1882

Knight Surname Ireland: 1600s to 1900s

Anastasia Hanrick, daughter of Philip Hanrick (daughter-in-law):

  Residence - 5 Dargle Road, Drumcondra - June 12, 1882

Philip Hanrick (father):

  Occupation - Corn Merchant

Joshua George Knight (father):

  Occupation - Watch Maker

- Lawrence Knight & Mary Unknown

  - Michael Knight – bapt. 22 Sep 1742 (Baptism, **St. Nicholas Parish (RC)**)

  - Catherine Knight – bapt. 24 Nov 1743 (Baptism, **St. Nicholas Parish (RC)**)

- Michael Knight & Bridget McEvoy

  - Lucy Knight – b. 16 Jun 1875, bapt. 24 Jun 1875 (Baptism, **SS. Michael & John Parish**

    (RC))

Michael Knight (father):

  Residence - 16 Essex Quay - June 24, 1875

- Michael Knight & Delia Corbit

  - Mary Knight – b. 15 Feb 1842, bapt. 15 Feb 1842 (Baptism, **Boherbue Parish (RC)**)

Michael Knight (father):

  Residence - Glounreagh - February 15, 1842

- Michael Francis Knight & Lucretia McCull – 2 May 1854 (Marriage, **Cork - SS. Peter & Paul**

  Parish (RC))

  - Mary Knight – bapt. 11 Mar 1855 (Baptism, **Cork - South Parish (RC)**)

- Nicholas Knight & Jane Dungan – 25 Nov 1655 (Marriage, **St. Michan Parish**)

- Nicholas Knight & Unknown

  - Oliver Knight – bur. 17 Feb 1656 (Burial, **St. John Parish**)

Hurst

- Nicholas Knight, d. 10 May 1731, bur. 12 May 1731 (Burial, **St. Nicholas Within Parish**) (Burial, **St. Nicholas Without Parish**) & Catherine Knight, bur. 1 Jan 1730 (Burial, **St. Nicholas Within Parish**) (Burial, **St. Nicholas Without Parish**)

Nicholas Knight (husband):

Remarks about Occupation - The church register reads as follows:

"The Rev. Mr. Knight appointed curate of St. Nicholas within 12th May, 1730."

Remarks about Burial - The church register entry reads as follows:

"1731 - May 12. Nicholas Knight, D.D., Curate, died 10 May, buried 12th May. 1 Year in his appointment."

Catherine Knight (wife):

Remarks about Burial - The church register entry reads as follows:

"1730 - January 1. Mrs. Catherine Knight in the Chancel wife of Dr. Knight, curate of the Parish of St. Nicholas within."

- Patrick Knight & Julia Unknown

    o John Knight – bapt. 1851 (Baptism, **St. Mary, Haddington Road Parish (RC)**)

- Peter Knight & Elizabeth Gibney

    o Rose Knight – bapt. 1 May 1826 (Baptism, **St. Michan Parish (RC)**)

- Peter Knight & Unknown

    o John Knight – bapt. 24 Nov 1689 (Baptism, **St. John Parish**)

- Rainsford Knight & Honora Knight

    o Mark Sanders Knight – bapt. 9 Sep 1817 (Baptism, **St. Mary Parish**)

- Richard Knight & Anne Knight

    o Richard Thomas Knight – b. 1 Mar 1825, bapt. 13 Mar 1825 (Baptism, **Irishtown Parish**)

Knight Surname Ireland: 1600s to 1900s

- Richard Knight & Anne Unknown

  o Edward Knight – b. 27 Mar 1827, bapt. 8 Apr 1827 (Baptism, **St. Matthew Parish**)

Richard Knight (father):

Residence - Ringsend - April 8, 1827

Occupation - Fisherman - April 8, 1827

- Richard Knight & Bridget Unknown

  o Anne Knight – bapt. 1834 (Baptism, **St. Andrew Parish (RC)**)

- Richard Knight & Catherine Knight

  o John Knight – bapt. 9 Mar 1697 (Baptism, **St. Michan Parish**), bur. 25 Jun 1698 (Burial, **St. Michan Parish**)

  o Elizabeth Knight – bur. 29 Jun 1699 (Burial, **St. Michan Parish**)

Richard Knight (father):

Occupation - Poulterer - March 9, 1697

June 25, 1698

June 29, 1699

- Richard Knight & Elizabeth Knight, bur. 15 Jun 1696 (Burial, **St. Michan Parish**)

Richard Knight (husband):

Occupation - Poulterer - June 15, 1696

- Richard Knight & Elizabeth Knight

  o William Knight – bapt. 28 Mar 1779 (Baptism, **St. Luke Parish**)

  o Richard Knight – bapt. 23 Apr 1780 (Baptism, **St. Luke Parish**)

Richard Knight (father):

Residence - New Row - March 28, 1779

April 23, 1780

Occupation - Shoemaker - March 28, 1779

April 23, 1780

Hurst

- Richard Knight & Esther Unknown

  o Anne Knight – bapt. 2 Dec 1753 (Baptism, **St. Nicholas Without Parish**)

Richard Knight (father):

Residence - Patrick Street - December 2, 1753

- Richard Knight & Honora Sullivan

  o Michael Knight – bapt. 5 Sep 1857 (Baptism, **Murragh & Templemartin Parish (RC)**)

- Richard Knight & Jane Browne – 25 May 1826 (Marriage, **St. Peter Parish**)

Richard Knight (husband):

Residence - Fitzwilliam Square - May 25, 1826

Jane Browne (wife):

Residence - St. Peter's Parish - May 25, 1826

Relationship Status at Marriage - widow

- Richard Knight & Jane Conner – 3 Apr 1743 (Marriage, **St. Anne Parish**)

- Richard Knight & Jane McVaugh – 8 Mar 1795 (Marriage, **St. Anne Parish**)

- Richard Knight & Jane Unknown

  o Sarah Knight – b. 1824, bapt. 1824 (Baptism, **Chapelizod Parish**)

- Richard Knight & Jane Whape – 26 Jan 1745 (Marriage, **St. Michan Parish**)

Richard Knight (husband):

Occupation - Linen Draper - January 26, 1745

- Richard Knight & Julia Knight

  o Mary Jane Knight – bapt. 10 Jul 1826 (Baptism, **St. Mary, Pro Cathedral Parish (RC)**)

Richard Knight (father):

Residence - Gloster Place - July 10, 1826

Knight Surname Ireland: 1600s to 1900s

- Richard Knight & Margaret Redmond – 10 Mar 1731 (Marriage, **St. Michan Parish**)

Richard Knight (husband):

  Occupation - Tinman - March 10, 1731

Margaret Redmond (wife):

  Relationship Status at Marriage - widow

- Richard Knight & Mary Bradford

    o   Martha Knight – bapt. 28 Jul 1745 (Baptism, **St. Catherine Parish (RC)**)

- Richard Knight & Mary Knight

    o   Richard Knight – b. 17 Mar 1853, bapt. 15 Aug 1856 (Baptism, **St. Michan Parish (RC)**)

Richard Knight (father):

  Residence - Santry - August 15, 1856

- Richard Knight & Mary Timmons

    o   Clare Mary Knight – b. 19 Dec 1897, bapt. 7 Jan 1898 (Baptism, **St. Mary, Pro Cathedral Parish (RC)**)

Richard Knight (father):

  Residence - 28 Great Charles Street - January 7, 1898

- Richard Knight & Mary White – 7 Oct 1817 (Marriage, **St. Mary Parish**)

- Richard Knight & Unknown

    o   Hester Knight – bapt. 6 Feb 1770 (Baptism, **St. Patrick Parish**)

- Robert Knight & Catherine Unknown

    o   Edward Knight – bapt. 17 Feb 1813 (Baptism, **St. Peter Parish**)

Robert Knight (father):

  Residence - Upper Baggot Street - February 17, 1813

Hurst

- Robert Knight & Elizabeth Maher

  - Mary Knight – b. 10 Feb 1868, bapt. 13 Feb 1868 (Baptism, **SS. Michael & John Parish (RC)**)

  - Elizabeth Knight – b. 9 Jun 1870, bapt. 20 Jun 1870 (Baptism, **SS. Michael & John Parish (RC)**)

Robert Knight (father):

Residence - 3 Back Lane - February 13, 1868

4 Back Lane - June 20, 1870

- Robert Knight & Elizabeth Margaret Unknown

  - Mary Knight – bapt. 20 Feb 1698 (Baptism, **St. Peter Parish**)

  - Unknown Knight – bapt. 16 Dec 1700 (Baptism, **St. Peter Parish**)

  - Anne Knight – bapt. 1 Feb 1702 (Baptism, **St. Peter Parish**)

  - William Knight – bapt. 22 Jul 1704 (Baptism, **St. Peter Parish**)

Robert Knight (father):

Residence - Kevin's Port - February 20, 1698

December 16, 1700

February 1, 1702

July 22, 1704

- Robert Knight & Jane Knight

  - Robert Knight – bapt. 11 Dec 1785 (Baptism, **St. Paul Parish**)

- Robert Knight & Louisa Knight

  - Emily Mary Knight – bapt. 15 Sep 1850 (Baptism, **Arbour Hill Barracks Parish**)

Robert Knight (father):

Residence - Royal Barracks - September 15, 1850

Occupation - Regiment's Sergeant Major 12th Royal Lancers -

September 15, 1850

Knight Surname Ireland: 1600s to 1900s

- Robert Knight & Mary Knight

  o Sarah Knight – bapt. 4 Feb 1849 (Baptism, **Arbour Hill Barracks Parish**)

Robert Knight (father):

Residence - Linen Hall Barracks - February 4, 1849

Occupation - Private 1st Royals - February 4, 1849

- Robert Knight & Mary Knight

  o John Knight – b. 1866, bapt. Jul 1871 (Baptism, **Irishtown Parish**), bur. 29 Jan 1872

  (Burial, **Irishtown Parish**)

John Knight (son):

Residence - Ringsend - Before January 29, 1872

Age at Death - 6 years

  o Robert Knight – b. 28 Jul 1871, bapt. Jul 1871 (Baptism, **Irishtown Parish**), bur. 29 Jul

  1871 (Burial, **Irishtown Parish**)

Robert Knight (son):

Residence - Ringsend - Before July 29, 1871

Age at Death - 1 day

  o Henrietta Knight & Alexander Little – 16 Nov 1891 (Marriage, **Irishtown Parish**)

Signatures:

Henrietta Knight (daughter):

   Residence - 2 York Terrace - November 16, 1891

Alexander Little, son of John Little (son-in-law):

   Residence - 6 Pigeon House Road - November 16, 1891

   Occupation - Bottleblower - November 16, 1891

   Relationship Status at Marriage - minor

John Little (father):

   Occupation - Glass Manufacturer

Robert Knight (father):

   Occupation - Fisherman

   o   Martha Knight – b. 1 Jun 1874, bapt. 21 Jun 1874 (Baptism, **Irishtown Parish**)

Signature:

   o   Elizabeth Knight – b. 17 Jan 1878, bapt. 29 Jan 1879 (Baptism, **Irishtown Parish**)

Robert Knight (father):

   Residence - Ringsend - July 1871

                        June 21, 1874

                        January 29, 1879

   Occupation - Fisherman - July 1871

                        June 21, 1874

                        January 29, 1879

- Robert Knight & Susannah Knight

   o   Margaret Knight – bapt. 10 Oct 1802 (Baptism, **St. Mary Parish**)

Knight Surname Ireland: 1600s to 1900s

- Samuel Knight & Elizabeth Knight

  o Caroline Knight – b. 11 Feb 1875, bapt. 14 Feb 1875 (Baptism, **Rotunda Chapel Parish**)

Samuel Knight (father):

Residence - 12 Lower Georges, Kingstown - February 14, 1875

Occupation - Seaman - February 14, 1875

- Samuel Knight & Elizabeth Palmer

  o James Knight – bapt. 15 Mar 1849 (Baptism, **Courcy's Country or Ballinspittal Parish (RC)**)

  o John Knight – bapt. 9 Sep 1850 (Baptism, **Courcy's Country or Ballinspittal Parish (RC)**)

  o Jane Knight – bapt. 17 Oct 1853 (Baptism, **Courcy's Country or Ballinspittal Parish (RC)**)

  o Anne Knight – bapt. 31 Jun 1855 (Baptism, **Courcy's Country or Ballinspittal Parish (RC)**)

  o Mary Knight – bapt. 19 Mar 1857 (Baptism, **Courcy's Country or Ballinspittal Parish (RC)**)

  o Mary Knight – bapt. 11 Jan 1859 (Baptism, **Courcy's Country or Ballinspittal Parish (RC)**)

  o Christopher Knight – bapt. 12 Jun 1861 (Baptism, **Courcy's Country or Ballinspittal Parish (RC)**)

  o Susanna Knight – bapt. 25 May 1865 (Baptism, **Courcy's Country or Ballinspittal Parish (RC)**)

  o Mary Knight – bapt. 28 Jul 1867 (Baptism, **Courcy's Country or Ballinspittal Parish (RC)**)

- o Samuel Knight – bapt. 28 Mar 1869 (Baptism, **Courcy's Country or Ballinspittal Parish (RC)**)

- Samuel Knight & Mary Walsh

  - o Samuel Knight & Catherine Leahy – 21 Sep 1879 (Marriage, **St. Mary, Pro Cathedral Parish (RC)**)

Samuel Knight (son):

    Residence - 6 Great Britain Street - September 21, 1879

Catherine Leahy, daughter of Anselm Leahy & Mary Maher (daughter-in-law):

    Residence - 6 Great Britain Street - September 21, 1879

Anselm Leahy (father):

    Residence - Kilkenny

Samuel Knight (father):

    Residence - Kilkenny

- Samuel Knight & Susan Unknown

  - o Joseph Skearing Knight – b. 30 Aug 1845, bapt. 14 Sep 1845 (Baptism, **St. Peter Parish**)

Samuel Knight (father):

    Residence - Richmond Place - September 14, 1845

    Occupation - Carpet - September 14, 1845

- Samuel Knight & Unknown

  - o Catherine Knight & James Colthurst – 20 Dec 1873 (Marriage, **Rathmines Parish**)

Signatures:

Knight Surname Ireland: 1600s to 1900s

Catherine Knight (daughter):

    Residence - Tullow, Co. Waterford - December 20, 1873

James Colthurst, son of James Colthurst (son-in-law):

    Residence - Rochestown, Cork - December 20, 1873

        16 Leinster Road - December 20, 1873

    Occupation - Esquire - December 20, 1873

    Relationship Status at Marriage - widow

James Colthurst (father):

    Occupation - Captain in Army

Samuel Knight (father):

    Occupation - Carpenter

- Simon Knight & Anne Unknown

  - Bridget Knight & Edward Robinson – 13 Aug 1863 (Marriage, **St. Michan Parish (RC)**)

    - Jane Robinson – b. 3 Mar 1859, bapt. 9 Mar 1859 (Baptism, **St. Michan Parish (RC)**)

    - Frances Mary Robinson – b. 5 Jan 1861, bapt. 9 Jan 1861 (Baptism, **St. Michan Parish (RC)**)

    - Henry Arthur Robinson – b. 13 Jul 1866, bapt. 23 Jul 1866 (Baptism, **St. Michan Parish (RC)**)

Bridget Knight (daughter):

    Residence - 30 Montpelier Hill - August 13, 1863

Edward Robinson, son of Garrett Robinson & Joan Unknown (son-in-law):

    Residence - 36 Bolton Street - March 9, 1859

        51 Dominick Street - January 9, 1861

        July 23, 1866

        30 Montpelier Hill - August 13, 1863

        Co. Kildare - August 13, 1863

- Simon Knight & Ellen Whelan – 10 Nov 1855 (Marriage, **Chapelizod Parish (RC)**)

Hurst

- Stephen Knight & Sarah Knight

  o Ellen Knight – b. 22 Jul 1844, bapt. 7 Mar 1875 (Baptism, **Arbour Hill Barracks Parish**)

Stephen Knight (father):

Residence - Royal Barracks - March 7, 1875

Occupation - Sergeant Face of 6th Innis Kings - March 7, 1875

- Thomas Knight & Anne Knight

  o John Knight – bapt. 20 May 1798 (Baptism, **St. Mark Parish**)

  o Sarah Knight – bapt. 18 Nov 1799 (Baptism, **St. Mark Parish**)

  o Margaret Knight – bapt. 19 Jul 1801 (Baptism, **St. Mark Parish**)

  o George Knight – bapt. 5 Sep 1802 (Baptism, **St. Mark Parish**)

Thomas Knight (father):

Residence - Townsend Street - May 20, 1798

November 18, 1799

87 Townsend Street - July 19, 1801

107 Townsend Street - September 5, 1802

- Thomas Knight & Anne White – 3 Aug 1783 (Marriage, **St. Mark Parish**)

  o Richard Knight – bapt. 13 Jun 1784 (Baptism, **St. Mark Parish**)

  o Frederick Knight – bapt. 31 Dec 1786 (Baptism, **St. Mark Parish**)

  o Mary Anne Knight – bapt. 5 May 1788 (Baptism, **St. Mark Parish**)

  o Esther Knight – bapt. 13 Nov 1789 (Baptism, **St. Mark Parish**)

  o Thomas Knight – bapt. 29 Mar 1791 (Baptism, **St. Mark Parish**)

  o Elizabeth Knight – bapt. 25 Feb 1793 (Baptism, **St. Mark Parish**)

  o Elizabeth Knight – bapt. 26 Sep 1796 (Baptism, **St. Mark Parish**)

Knight Surname Ireland: 1600s to 1900s

Thomas Knight (father):

Residence - College Street - June 13, 1784

Lazer's Hill - December 31, 1786

May 5, 1788

November 13, 1789

March 29, 1791

February 25, 1793

September 26, 1796

- Thomas Knight & Christian Ffourd – 1 Apr 1703 (Marriage, **St. Michan Parish**)

Thomas Knight (husband):

Occupation - Brewer - April 1, 1703

- Thomas Knight & Eleanor Halpin

  o   Mary Anne Knight – bapt. 28 Dec 1828 (Baptism, **St. Catherine Parish (RC)**)

- Thomas Knight & Elizabeth Maidment – 16 Apr 1840 (Marriage, **St. Paul Parish**)

Signatures:

- Thomas Knight & Frances Knight

  o   Eleanor Knight – b. 14 Aug 1887, bapt. 31 Aug 1887 (Baptism, **St. Werburgh Parish**)

Thomas Knight (father):

Residence - Ship Street Barracks - August 31, 1887

Occupation - Sergeant West York Regiment - August 31, 1887

- Thomas Knight & Margaret Brophy

  o   Honora Knight – bapt. 12 Feb 1839 (Baptism, **St. Michan Parish (RC)**)

Hurst

- Thomas Knight & Mary Knight

  o James Knight – bapt. 25 Nov 1688 (Baptism, **St. Michan Parish**)

Thomas Knight (father):

  Occupation - Carman - November 25, 1688

- Thomas Knight & Mary Knight

  o Joseph Francis Knight – b. 6 May 1856, bapt. 6 Apr 1857 (Baptism, **St. Mary Parish**)

Thomas Knight (father):

  Residence - 63 Jervis Street - April 6, 1857

  Occupation - Glove Cleaner - April 6, 1857

- Thomas Knight & Mary Knight

  o Mary Ellen Knight – b. 22 May 1882, bapt. 7 Jun 1882 (Baptism, **Portobello Barracks Parish**)

Thomas Knight (father):

  Residence - 4 Carlisle Terrace Grand Canal - June 7, 1882

  Occupation - Gunner Royal Horse Artillery - June 7, 1882

- Thomas Knight & Mary Knight

  o Thomas Knight – b. 16 Dec 1883, bapt. 13 Jan 1884 (Baptism, **Portobello Barracks Parish**)

Thomas Knight (father):

  Residence - Dublin - January 13, 1884

  Occupation - Garrison Butcher - January 13, 1884

- Thomas Knight & Mary Lane – 30 Nov 1688 (Marriage, **St. Michael Parish**)

- Thomas Knight & Mary Maloney

  o Mary Ellen Knight – bapt. 1886 (Baptism, **St. Andrew Parish** (RC))

Thomas Knight (father):

  Residence - Gresham Hotel, O'Connell Street - 1866

Knight Surname Ireland: 1600s to 1900s

- Thomas Knight & Mary Quinn

  o Mary Ellen Knight – b. 1882, bapt. 1882 (Baptism, **St. Andrew Parish (RC)**)

Thomas Knight (father):

Residence - 3 Clarendon Row - 1882

- Thomas Knight & Mary Unknown

  o John Knight – b. 22 Mar 1836, bapt. 3 Apr 1836 (Baptism, **Taney Parish**)

  o Thomas Knight – b. 28 Oct 1837, bapt. 12 Nov 1837 (Baptism, **St. Peter Parish**)

  o Catherine Knight – b. 10 Sep 1839, bapt. 13 Oct 1839 (Baptism, **St. Peter Parish**)

  o Anne Knight – b. 6 Feb 1842, bapt. 20 Feb 1842 (Baptism, **St. Peter Parish**)

Thomas Knight (father):

Residence - Dublin - April 3, 1836

58 Upper Kevin Street - November 12, 1837

12 Upper Kevin Street - October 13, 1839

6 Bishop Street - February 20, 1842

Occupation - Writing Clerk - April 3, 1836

February 20, 1842

- Thomas Knight & Mary Jane Kenny

  o Catherine Mary Josephine Knight – b. 31 May 1889, bapt. 3 Jun 1889 (Baptism, **St. Mary, Donnybrook Parish (RC)**)

Thomas Knight (father):

Residence - 40 Marlboro Road - June 3, 1889

- Thomas Knight & Rebecca Hiorn (H i o r n) – 5 Mar 1715 (Baptism, **St. John Parish**)

- Thomas Knight & Unknown

Signature:

- ○ Catherine Knight & James Lord – 26 Nov 1860 (Marriage, **St. Luke Parish**)

Signatures:

- ▪ Mary Catherine Lord – b. 1865, bapt. 1865 (Baptism, **St. Andrew Parish (RC)**)

Catherine Knight (daughter):

> Residence - 36 New Row - November 26, 1860

> Occupation - Painter - November 26, 1860

James Lord, son of Lawrence Lord (son-in-law):

> Residence - New Row - November 26, 1860

>> 39 Dame Street - 1865

> Occupation - Painter - November 26, 1860

Lawrence Lord (father):

> Occupation - Laborer

Thomas Knight (father):

> Occupation - Glover

Wedding Witnesses:

Thomas Knight & Elizabeth Kenesown

Signatures:

- Thomas Knight & Unknown

  o William Knight & Judith Stratford – 11 Sep 1865 (Marriage, **Clontarf Parish**)

Signatures:

William Knight (son):

    Residence - Bierly's Baths, Clontarf, Co. Dublin - September 11, 1865

        Corquill, Co. Cavin - September 11, 1865

    Occupation - Farmer - September 11, 1865

Judith Stratford, daughter of Thomas Stratford (daughter-in-law):

    Residence - Coolboy, Drumhummon Granard Parish - September 11, 1865

    Relationship Status at Marriage - minor

Thomas Stratford (father):

    Occupation - Farmer

Thomas Knight (father):

    Occupation - Farmer

- Thomas Knight & Unknown

Signature:

- ○ Anne Knight & Michael Crowe – 26 Dec 1866 (Marriage, **St. Andrew Parish**)

Signatures:

- ▪ Mary Anne Crowe – b. 1 Jun 1868, bapt. 15 Jun 1868 (Baptism, **St. Mary, Pro**

  Cathedral Parish (RC))

Anne Knight (daughter):

Residence - 39 Dame Street - December 26, 1866

Occupation - Tailoress - December 26, 1866

Michael Crowe, son of Michael Crowe (son-in-law):

Residence - 39 Dame Street - December 26, 1866

30 Mabbot Street - June 15, 1868

Occupation - Tailor - December 26, 1866

Michael Crowe (father):

Occupation - Brickmaker

Thomas Knight (father):

Occupation - Messenger

Wedding Witnesses:

Thomas Knight & John Knight

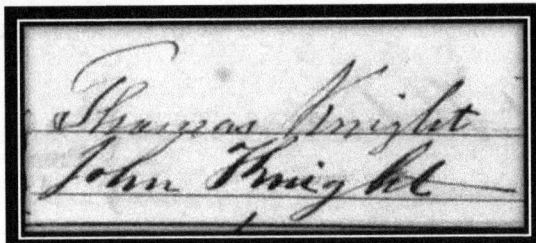

Signatures:

- Thomas Knight & Unknown

  o Joseph Knight & Anne Boothman Malone – 18 Dec 1876 (Marriage, **St. Peter Parish**)

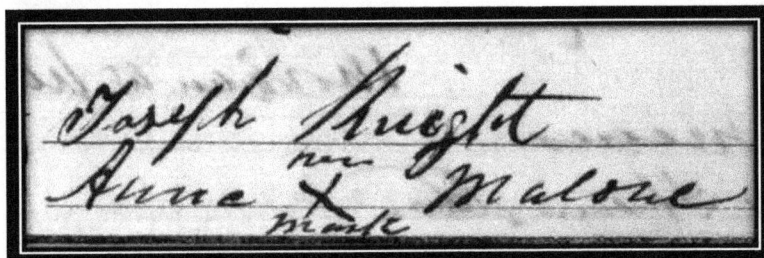

Signatures:

Joseph Knight (son):

    Residence - 23 Upper Camden Street - December 18, 1876

    Occupation - Organ Builder - December 18, 1876

    Relationship Status at Marriage - widow

Anne Boothman Malone, daughter of John Boothman (daughter-in-law):

    Residence - 31 Charlemont Street - December 18, 1876

    Occupation - Straw Bonnet Maker - December18, 1876

John Boothman (father):

    Occupation - Carpenter

Thomas Knight (father):

    Occupation - Car Owner

Hurst

- Thomas Newcomen Knight & Jane Brabzon – 8 Nov 1688 (Marriage, **St. Michan Parish**)

- Unknown Knight, d. Before 30 May 1740 & Eleanor Knight

    - Catherine Knight – bapt. 30 May 1740 (Baptism, **St. Michan Parish (RC)**)

Eleanor Knight (mother):

Residence - Market - May 30, 1740

- Unknown Knight & Ellen Coole

    - Timothy Knight – bapt. Nov 1814 (Baptism, **Kilbrittain Parish (RC)**)

- Unknown Knight & Ellen Mane

    - Lucy Knight – bapt. 1864 (Baptism, **Chapelizod Parish (RC)**)

Unknown Knight (father):

Residence - Chapelizod - 1864

- Unknown Knight & Unknown

    - Unknown Knight (child) – bur. 4 Nov 1691 (Burial, **St. John Parish**)

Unknown Knight (father):

Occupation - Silkman - November 4, 1691

- Walter Knight & Anne Knight

    - Walter Sadoolapose Knight – b. 3 Dec 1859, bapt. 25 Jan 1859 (Baptism, **Portobello Barracks Parish**)

Walter Knight (father):

Residence - Portobello Barracks - January 25, 1859

Occupation - Corporal 3rd Light Dragoons - January 25, 1859

- Walter Knight & Elizabeth Byrne (B y r n e) – 7 Jun 1818 (Marriage, **St. James Parish**)

Knight Surname Ireland: 1600s to 1900s

- Wellesley John Giles Knight & Unknown

  - William Thomas Knight & Elizabeth Charlotte Lord – 19 Sep 1900 (Marriage, **St. Catherine Parish**)

Signatures:

William Thomas Knight (son):

    Residence - 78 South Great George's Street - September 19, 1900

    Occupation - Clerk - September 19, 1900

Elizabeth Charlotte Lord, daughter of George Lord (daughter-in-law):

    Residence - 27 St. Albans Road South Circular Road - September 19, 1900

George Lord (father):

    Occupation - School Master

Wellesley John Giles Knight (father):

    Occupation - School Master

- Wesley Knight & Unknown

  - Amelia Christina Knight & William Alexander Maffatt – 29 Aug 1898 (Marriage, **Sandford Parish**)

Amelia Christina Knight (daughter):

    Residence - The Schoolhouse, Sandford - August 29, 1898

William Alexander Maffatt, son of Thomas Maffatt (son-in-law):

    Residence - 2 Chelmsford Road - August 29, 1898

    Occupation - Draper - August 29, 1898

Hurst

Thomas Maffatt (father):

    Occupation - Clerk

Wesley Knight (father):

    Occupation - School Master

Wedding Witnesses:

William Bell Knight & Eva Knight

- William Knight & Catherine Rice – 27 Jun 1790 (Marriage, **St. Michan Parish (RC)**)

- William Knight & Catherine Unknown

  - Mary Knight – bapt. 23 Nov 1728 (Baptism, **St. Michan Parish (RC)**)

William Knight (father):

    Residence - Frappers Lane - November 23, 1728

- William Knight & Catherine Unknown

  - Anne Knight – bapt. 29 Aug 1734 (Baptism, **St. Nicholas Without Parish**)

William Knight (father):

    Residence - Patrick Street - August 29, 1734

- William Knight & Clara Knight

  - Albert Ernest (E r n e s t) Victor Knight – b. 20 Sep 1888, bapt. 21 Sep 1888 (Baptism,

    Arbour Hill Barracks Parish) (Baptism, **St. Paul Parish**)

William Knight (father):

    Residence - Royal Barracks - September 21, 1888

    Occupation - Officer's Mess Caterer 5th Dragoon Guards - September 21, 1888

        Sergeant Major - September 21, 1888

- William Knight & Emily C. Harvey

  - George Henry Knight – b. 14 Sep 1905, bapt. 3 Jun 1906 (Baptism, **Dingle Parish**)

  - Kenneth H. Knight – b. 20 Oct 1906, bapt. 7 Jul 1907 (Baptism, **Dingle Parish**)

William Knight (father):

Residence - Coast Guard Station, Ventry - June 3, 1906

Knight Surname Ireland: 1600s to 1900s

- William Knight & Hannah Unknown

  - William Knight – bapt. 20 Aug 1781 (Baptism, **St. Catherine Parish**)

William Knight (father):

Residence - Tripelo - August 20, 1781

- William Knight & Jane Jones

  - Christopher Knight – b. 1859, bapt. 1885

William Knight (father):

Residence - 19 East James Street - 1885

- William Knight & Jane Knight

  - William Knight – bapt. 18 Jan 1824 (Baptism, **St. Paul Parish**)

- William Knight & Jane Knight

  - Christopher Arbsted Knight – b. 21 Mar 1860, bapt. 5 Aug 1860 (Baptism, **St. Peter Parish**)

William Knight (father):

Residence - 26 New Bride Street - August 5, 1860

Occupation - House Painter - August 5, 1860

- William Knight & Jane Knight

  - Henry Knight – b. 24 Mar 1863, bapt. 6 Mar 1864 (Baptism, **St. Peter Parish**)

William Knight (father):

Residence - 48 Lower Baggot Street - March 6, 1864

Occupation - Artist - March 6, 1864

- William Knight & Jane Robinson – 16 Aug 1674 (Marriage, **St. Andrew Parish**)

Hurst

- William Knight & Jane Unknown

  - Henry Knight & Elizabeth Mantle – 27 Jul 1885 (Marriage, **Sandford Parish**)

    - Elizabeth Maud Knight – b. 1886, bapt. 1886 (Baptism, **Sandford Parish**)

    - Evelyn Winifred Knight – b. 1887, bapt. 1887 (Baptism, **Sandford Parish**)

    - Florence Jane Knight – b. 1889, bapt. 1889 (Baptism, **Sandford Parish**)

    - Henry Joseph Knight – b. 26 Jul 1891, bapt. 6 Sep 1891 (Baptism, **St. Catherine Parish**)

    - Eileen Knight – b. 18 Aug 1893, bapt. 16 Sep 1893 (Baptism, **St. Catherine Parish**)

Henry Knight (son):

Residence - 3 Mount Pleasant Avenue - July 27, 1885

21 Annavilla - 1886

25 Annavilla - 1887

25 Annavilla Cullenwood - 1889

5 Susan Terrace - September 6, 1891

66 Eugene Street - September 16, 1893

Occupation - House Painter - July 27, 1885

1889

Painter - 1886

1887

September 6, 1891

September 16, 1893

Elizabeth Mantle, daughter of Joseph Mantle (daughter-in-law):

Residence - Woodstock Lodge, Sandford Road - July 27, 1885

Joseph Mantle (father):

Occupation - Gardener

William Knight (father):

Occupation - House Painter

Wedding Witnesses:

Joseph mantle & John Carron

Knight Surname Ireland: 1600s to 1900s

- Charles Harris Brady Knight – b. 12 Jun 1865, bapt. 12 Oct 1865 (Baptism, **St. Stephen Parish**)

- Mary Kingsmill Knight, b. 1 Nov 1866, bapt. 6 Dec 1866 (Baptism, **St. Stephen Parish**) & Thomas Henry Moore – 7 Mar 1889 (Marriage, **Sandford Parish**)

Mary Kingsmill Knight (daughter):

   Residence - **25 Annavilla Avenue - March 7, 1889**

Thomas Henry Moore, son of Henry Moore (son-in-law):

   Residence - **7 Ebenezer Terrace - March 7, 1889**

   Occupation - **Engine Driver - March 7, 1889**

Henry Moore (father):

   Occupation - **Cab Owner**

William Knight (father):

   Occupation - **Employer**

- Henrietta Knight – b. 28 Feb 1869, bapt. 25 Mar 1869 (Baptism, **St. Stephen Parish**)

- Jane Knight – b. 22 Sep 1871, bapt. 22 Feb 1872 (Baptism, **St. Stephen Parish**)

- Wilhelmina Knight – b. 1 Nov 1873, bapt. 26 Feb 1874 (Baptism, **St. Stephen Parish**)

- William Knight – b. 29 Jan 1876, bapt. 5 Jun 1876 (Baptism, **St. Stephen Parish**)

- Charles Heinz Brady Knight – b. 15 Feb 1879, bapt. 17 May 1881 (Baptism, **St. Stephen Parish**)

- Thomas Desmond Knight – b. Jun 1881, bapt. 19 Dec 1884 (Baptism, **St. Stephen Parish**)

- Sarah Maud Knight – b. Nov 1884, bapt. 19 Dec 1884 (Baptism, **St. Stephen Parish**)

Hurst

William Knight (father):

Residence - 19 East James Street - December 6, 1866

March 25, 1869

February 22, 1872

February 26, 1874

June 5, 1876

May 17, 1881

December 19, 1884

Occupation - Contractor - December 6, 1866

Painter - October 12, 1865

March 25, 1869

May 17, 1881

December 19, 1884

House Painter - February 22, 1872

February 26, 1874

June 5, 1876

- William Knight & Julia Knight

  o Anne Mary Sophia Nelson Knight – b. 2 Aug 1821, bapt. 13 Aug 1821 (Baptism, St. Mark Parish)

- William Knight & Margaret Knight

  o Sarah Knight – bapt. 10 Nov 1782 (Baptism, St. Paul Parish)

- William Knight & Margaret McGovernan (M c G o v e r n a n)

  o William Knight – bapt. 24 Mar 1833 (Baptism, Kinsale Parish (RC))

Knight Surname Ireland: 1600s to 1900s

- William Knight & Mary Knight

  - Lydia Knight – bapt. 1 Mar 1783 (Baptism, **St. Audoen Parish**)

  - Sarah Knight – bapt. 29 Jan 1785 (Baptism, **St. Audoen Parish**)

  - John Knight – bapt. 27 Jan 1786 (Baptism, **St. Audoen Parish**)

  - John Knight – bapt. 21 Sep 1794 (Baptism, **St. Audoen Parish**)

- William Knight & Mary Knight

  - Henry Knight – bapt. 16 Sep 1839 (Baptism, **Castleisland Parish**)

William Knight (father):

Residence - Castleisland - September 16, 1839

Occupation - Innkeeper - September 16, 1839

- William Knight & Mary Jane Knight

  - Anne Mary Knight – b. 1 Jul 1845, bapt. 15 Jan 1846 (Baptism, **Dunleckney Parish**)

  - Belinda Emily Knight – b. 6 Nov 1847, bapt. 11 Feb 1848 (Baptism, **Dunleckney Parish**)

  - Loveday Catherine Knight – b. 1 Oct 1849, bapt. 4 Nov 1849 (Baptism, **Dunleckney Parish**)

  - Abraham William Knight – b. 19 Mar 1852, bapt. 4 May 1852 (Baptism, **Dunleckney Parish**)

  - Robert Homan (H o m a n) Knight – b. 15 Jul 1855, bapt. 23 Sep 1855 (Baptism, **Dunleckney Parish**)

Hurst

William Knight (father):

    Residence - Bagenalstown - January 15, 1846

                              February 11, 1848

                              November 4, 1849

                              May 4, 1852

                              September 23, 1855

    Occupation - Clerk - January 15, 1846

                              February 11, 1848

    Writing Clerk - November 4, 1849

                              May 4, 1852

                              September 23, 1855

- William Knight & Unknown

  o Elizabeth Knight – bapt. 15 Jun 1645 (Baptism, **St. John Parish**)

- William Knight & Unknown

Signature:

  o Anne Mary Knight & William Henry Lynn – 9 Feb 1866 (Marriage, **St. Peter Parish**)

Signatures:

Knight Surname Ireland: 1600s to 1900s

Anne Mary Knight (daughter):

    Residence - Kilbride Castle, Co. Westmeath - February 9, 1866

    Relationship Status at Marriage - minor

William Henry Lynn, son of Robert Lynn (son-in-law):

    Residence - 41 Synge Street, Steadbally, Queen's Co. - February 9, 1866

    Occupation - Clerk - February 9, 1866

Robert Lynn (father):

    Occupation - Esquire

William Knight (father):

    Occupation - Esquire

Wedding Witnesses:

William Knight & Richard Ludlow

Signatures:

Hurst

- William Knight & Unknown

    o Thomas Knight & Elizabeth Parsons – 22 Jun 1868 (Marriage, **St. Paul Parish**)

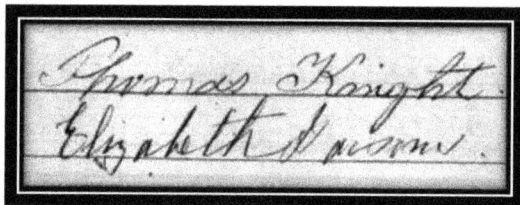

Signatures:

Thomas Knight (son):

    Residence - Island Bridge - June 22, 1868

    Occupation - Private in 6th Dragoons Guards - June 22, 1868

Elizabeth Parsons, daughter of James Parsons (daughter-in-law):

    Residence - Island Bridge - June 22, 1868

James Parsons (father):

    Occupation - Coach Man

William Knight (father):

    Occupation - Saddle Maker

- William Knight & Unknown

  o Samuel Nicholas Knight & Catherine Mary Unknown Gahan – 4 Jul 1881 (Marriage, St. Peter Parish)

Signatures:

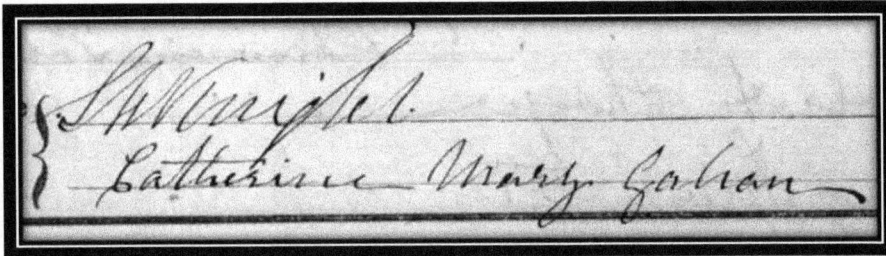

Samuel Nicholas Knight (son):

   Residence - 129 Lower George's Street, Kingstown - July 4, 1881

   Occupation - Government Clerk - July 4, 1881

   Relationship Status at Marriage - widow

Catherine Mary Unknown Gahan, daughter of Thomas Unknown

(daughter-in-law):

   Residence - 91 Harcourt Street - July 4, 1881

   Relationship Status at Marriage - widow

Thomas Unknown (father):

   Occupation - Dairyman

William Knight (father):

   Occupation - Grocer

- William Knight & Unknown

  o Wilhelmina Knight & Harold Chadwick Little – 30 Sep 1897 (Marriage, **St. Catherine Parish**)

Signatures:

Wilhelmina Knight (daughter):

    Residence - 23 Donore Avenue - September 30, 1897

Harold Chadwick Little, son of William Little (son-in-law):

    Residence - 14 Donnybrook Road - September 30, 1897

    Occupation - Plumber - September 30, 1897

William Little (father):

    Occupation - Painting Contractor

William Knight (father):

    Occupation - Painting Contractor

Wedding Witnesses:

George William Cunning Little and Jane Knight

Signatures:

Knight Surname Ireland: 1600s to 1900s

- William George Knight & Sarah Knight

  - William Henry Knight – b. 31 Jan 1889, bapt. 24 Mar 1889 (Baptism, **Kilmainham Parish**)

William George Knight (father):

Residence - Golden Bridge - March 24, 1889

Occupation - Private 2nd Battalion Scots Guards - March 24, 1889

- William Henry Knight & Mary Cronin – 19 May 1833 (Marriage, **Castleisland Parish (RC)**)

  - Charlotte Knight – b. 1 Apr 1837, bapt. 1 Apr 1837 (Baptism, **Castleisland Parish** (RC))

  - Honora Knight – b. 2 Jul 1838, bapt. 2 Jul 1838 (Baptism, **Castleisland Parish** (RC))

  - Samuel Knight – b. 3 May 1840, bapt. 3 May 1840 (Baptism, **Castleisland Parish** (RC))

William Henry Knight (father):

Residence - Castleisland - April 1, 1837

July 2, 1838

May 3, 1840

Individual Births/Baptisms

- Anne Knight – b. 1874, bapt. 28 Jun 1874 (Baptism, **St. James Parish** (RC))

- Bridget A. Knight – bapt. 27 Jan 1773 (Baptism, **St. Catherine Parish** (RC))

- Elizabeth Agnes Knight – b. 22 Jan 1897, bapt. 22 Jan 1897 (Baptism, **Tralee Parish** (RC))

- Mary Knight – b. 24 Jul 1898, bapt. 26 Jul 1898 (Baptism, **Rathmines Parish** (RC))

Mary Knight (child):

    Remarks at Birth - foundling

- Mary A. Knight – bapt. Jun 1854 (Baptism, **Cork - SS. Peter & Paul Parish** (RC))

- Matthew Knight – bapt. 3 Sep 1643 (Baptism, **St. John Parish**)

- Nicholas Knight – bapt. 8 Feb 1663 (Baptism, **St. John Parish**)

- Ruth Knight – bapt 5 Oct 1859 (Baptism, **Carlow Parish**), bur. 1859 (Burial, **Carlow Parish**)

Ruth Knight (child):

    Residence - Carlow - 1859

    Remarks at Baptism and Burial - foundling

Individual Burials

- Alexander Knight – bur. 29 Oct 1685 (Burial, **St. Audoen Parish**)

Alexander Knight (deceased):

> Residence - From Mr. Fuller - October 29, 1685

- Andrew Mee Knight – bur. 10 Jul 1740 (Burial, **St. John Parish**)

- Anne Knight – bur. 28 Dec 1712 (Burial, **St. Peter Parish**)

Anne Knight (deceased):

> Residence - Kevin's Port - Before December 28, 1712

- Anne Knight – bur. 1 Feb 1739 (Burial, **St. Luke Parish**)

- Anne Knight – bur. 26 Apr 1805 (Burial, **St. James Parish**)

Anne Knight (deceased):

> Residence - Usher's Quay - Before April 26, 1805

- Barbara Knight – b. Aug 1819, bur. 21 Aug 1819 (Burial, **St. Mark Parish**)

Barbara Knight (deceased):

> Residence - St. Nicholas Within Parish - Before August 21, 1819
>
> Age at Death - 2 weeks

- Catherine Knight – b. 1761, bur. 4 Dec 1841 (Burial, **St. Matthew Parish**)

Catherine Knight (deceased):

> Residence - Dublin - Before December 4, 1841
>
> Age at Death - 80 Years

- Christopher Knight – bur. 16 Apr 1813 (Burial, **St. James Parish**)

Christopher Knight (deceased):

> Residence - Poreford Street - Before April 16, 1813

Hurst

- Daniel Knight – bur. 18 Mar 1773 (Burial, **St. Paul Parish**)

Daniel Knight (deceased):

Residence - Aunfuir Street - Before March 18, 1773

- Edward Knight – bur. 11 Jan 1667 (Burial, **St. Michan Parish**)

- Edward Knight – bur. 19 Oct 1718 (Burial, **St. Paul Parish**)

- Edward Knight – bur. 7 Nov 1806 (Burial, **St. Mark Parish**)

- Eleanor Knight – bur. 4 Mar 1799 (Burial, **St. Paul Parish**)

- Elizabeth Knight – bur. 23 Feb 1672 (Burial, **St. Audoen Parish**)

Elizabeth Knight (deceased):

Social Status - a poor woman

- Elizabeth Knight – bur. 13 Feb 1698 (Burial, **St. Peter Parish**)

Elizabeth Knight (deceased):

Residence - Kevin's Port - Before February 13, 1698

- Elizabeth Knight – b. 1659, bur. 28 Mar 1715 (Burial, **St. Werburgh Parish**)

Elizabeth Knight (deceased):

Residence - Crane Lane - Before March 28, 1715

Age at Death - 56 years

Cause of Death - suddenly

- Elizabeth Knight – bur. 14 May 1728 (Burial, **St. Peter Parish**)

- Elizabeth Knight – bur. 11 Sep 1729 (Burial, **St. Paul Parish**)

- Elizabeth Knight – bur. 24 Sep 1816 (Burial, **St. Mark Parish**)

Elizabeth Knight (deceased):

Residence - White's Lane - Before September 24, 1816

- Elizabeth Knight – b. Jun 1843, bur. 16 Sep 1843 (Burial, **St. Catherine Parish**)

Elizabeth Knight (deceased):

Residence - 116 Thomas Street - Before September 16, 1843

Knight Surname Ireland: 1600s to 1900s

  Age at Death - 4 months

- Enoch Knight – bur. 4 Sep 1690 (Burial, **St. John Parish**)

- Esther Knight – bur. 18 Jul 1800 (Burial, **St. Paul Parish**)

- Francis John Knight – b. Aug 1869, d. 19 Sep 1869, bur. 29 Sep 1869 (Burial, **Arbour Hill**

  Barracks Parish)

Francis John Knight (deceased):

  Residence - Royal Barrack - September 19, 1869

  Age at Death - 6 weeks

  Remarks concerning Birth - not baptized

- George Knight – bur. 28 Jan 1631 (Burial, **St. John Parish**)

- George Knight – bur. 28 Feb 1675 (Burial, **St. John Parish**)

- George Knight (child) – bur. 10 Jan 1717 (Burial, **St. Catherine Parish**)

- George Knight – bur. 19 Mar 1725 (Burial, **St. Peter Parish**)

- George Knight – b. Jul 1837, bur. 9 Aug 1837 (Burial, **St. Matthew Parish**)

George Knight (deceased):

  Residence - Ringsend - Before August 9, 1837

  Age at Death - 2 weeks

- Henry Knight – bur. 3 Dec 1733 (Burial, **St. Peter Parish**)

- Henry Knight – b. 1804, bur. 11 Apr 1841 (Burial, **Ballymacelligott Parish**) (Burial,

  Castleisland Parish)

Henry Knight (deceased):

  Residence - Castleisland - Before April 11, 1841

  Age at Death - 37 years

- Honora Knight – b. 1793, bapt. 6 Sep 1844 (Burial, **St. Luke Parish**)

Honora Knight (deceased):

  Residence - Donnybrook - September 6, 1844

  Age at Death - 51 years

Hurst

- Humphrey Knight – bur. 12 Oct 1766 (Burial, **St. Mark Parish**)

Humphrey Knight (deceased):

> **Residence - George's Quay - Before October 12, 1766**

- James Knight – bur. 29 Apr 1685 (Burial, **St. John Parish**)

- James Knight – bur. 21 Aug 1740 (Burial, **St. Mary Parish**)

- Jane Knight – bur. 18 Apr 1693 (Burial, **St. Peter Parish**)

Jane Knight (deceased):

> **Residence - Love Lane - Before April 18, 1693**

- Jane Knight – bur. 28 Aug 1728 (Burial, **St. Nicholas Without Parish**)

- Jane Knight – bur. 7 Nov 1742 (Burial, **St. Paul Parish**)

- Jane Knight – b. 1763, bur. 14 Feb 1850 (Burial, **St. Mark Parish**)

Jane Knight (deceased):

> **Residence - 17 Marks Street - Before February 14, 1850**
> **Age at Death - 87 years**

- Jane Knight – b. 1789, bur. 17 Apr 1861 (Burial, **St. Peter Parish**)

Jane Knight (deceased):

> **Residence - 21 Upper Fitzwilliam Street - Before April 17, 1861**
> **Age at Death - 72 years**

- John Knight – bur. 22 Mar 1698 (Burial, **St. Catherine Parish**)

- John Knight (child) – bur. 4 Jul 1725 (Burial, **St. Catherine Parish**)

- John Knight – bur. 18 Feb 1727 (Burial, **St. Mary Parish**)

- John Knight – bur. 25 Jan 1729 (Burial, **St. Paul Parish**)

- John Knight – bur. 1 Dec 1737 (Burial, **St. Mark Parish**)

- John Knight – bur. 20 Nov 1772 (Burial, **St. Audoen Parish**)

- John Knight – bur. 23 Feb 1806 (Burial, **Glasnevin Parish**)

Knight Surname Ireland: 1600s to 1900s

- John Knight – bur. 27 Apr 1810 (Burial, **St. Nicholas Without Parish**)

John Knight (deceased):

> **Residence - Francis Street - Before April 27, 1810**

- John Knight – bur. 4 Sep 1726 (Burial, **St. Paul Parish**)

- John Franks Knight – b. 1769, bur. 14 Jan 1852 (Burial, **Taney Parish**)

John Franks Knight (deceased):

> **Residence - St. Bridget's Clonskeagh - Before January 14, 1852**
>
> **Age at Death - 83 years**

- Joseph Knight – bur. 1 Apr 1791 (Burial, **St. Paul Parish**)

- Joseph Knight – bur. 16 Nov 1805 (Burial, **St. Paul Parish**)

- Isaac Knight – bur. 29 Mar 1675 (Burial, **St. John Parish**)

- Isaac Knight – b. 1807, bur. 22 Apr 1828 (Burial, **St. Luke Parish**)

Isaac Knight (deceased):

> **Residence - Mary's Street - Before April 22, 1828**
>
> **Age at Death - 21 years**

- Isabel Knight – bur. 14 Jun 1725 (Burial, **St. Catherine Parish**)

- Lydia Knight – b. 1782, bur. 16 Aug 1818 (Burial, **St. Audoen Parish**)

Lydia Knight (deceased):

> **Residence - St. Audoen Parish - Before August 16, 1818**

- Mad Knight – bur. 22 Jun 1707 (Burial, **St. Peter Parish**)

Mad Knight (deceased):

> **Residence - Stephen's Green - Before June 22, 1707**

- Margaret Knight – bur. 23 Sep 1691 (Burial, **St. Peter Parish**)

Margaret Knight (deceased):

> **Residence - White Friars Street - Before September 23, 1691**

- Margaret Knight – bur. 20 Feb 1739 (Burial, **St. Luke Parish**)

Hurst

- Mark Knight – b. 1818, bur. 28 Mar 1830 (Burial, **St. Luke Parish**)

Mark Knight (deceased):

    Residence - Brittain Street - Before March 28, 1830

    Age at Death - 12 years

- Mary Knight – bur. 25 Sep 1696 (Burial, **St. Peter Parish**)

Mary Knight (deceased):

    Residence - Kevin's Street - Before September 25, 1696

- Mary Knight – bur. 5 Jun 1703 (Burial, **St. John Parish**)

Mary Knight (deceased):

    Relationship Status at Death - widow

- Mary Knight – bur. 4 Feb 1704 (Burial, **St. Nicholas Without Parish**)

Mary Knight (deceased):

    Residence - The Poddle - Before February 4, 1704

- Mary Knight – bur. 28 Apr 1714 (Burial, **St. Nicholas Without Parish**)

Mary Knight (deceased):

    Residence - Francis Street - Before April 28, 1714

- Mary Knight – bur. 30 Mar 1727 (Burial, **St. Paul Parish**)

- Mary Knight – bur. 4 Dec 1771 (Burial, **St. Michael Parish**)

Mary Knight (deceased):

    Residence - Michael's Lane - Before December 4, 1771

- Mary Knight – bur. 16 Sep 1772 (Burial, **St. Paul Parish**)

- Mary Knight – b. Mar 1847, bur. 4 Nov 1847 (Burial, **St. Peter Parish**)

Mary Knight (deceased):

    Residence - Church Lane - Before November 4, 1847

    Age at Death - 9 months

Knight Surname Ireland: 1600s to 1900s

- Mary Knight – b. 1804, bur. 31 Mar 1858 (Burial, **St. Mary Parish**)

Mary Knight (deceased):

> **Residence - 33 Jervis Street - Before March 31, 1858**
>
> **Age at Death - 54 years**

- Michael Knight – bur. 7 Jul 1669 (Burial, **St. Peter Parish**)

- Michael Knight – b. 1830, bur. 2 Oct 1832 (Burial, **St. Mark Parish**)

Michael Knight (deceased):

> **Residence - Townsend Street - Before October 2, 1832**
>
> **Age at Death - 2 years**

- Nathan Knight – bur. 1 Aug 1718 (Burial, **St. Paul Parish**)

- Paul Davis Knight – bur. 8 Dec 1672 (Burial, **St. Audoen Parish**)

- Peter Knight – b. 1831, bur. 25 Jul 1880 (Burial, **St. George Parish**)

Peter Knight (deceased):

> **Residence - Whitworth Hospital - Before July 25, 1880**
>
> **Age at Death - 49 years**

- Philip Knight – bur. 22 Jun 1714 (Burial, **St. Nicholas Without Parish**)

Philip Knight (deceased):

> **Residence - Francis Street - Before June 22, 1714**

- Ransford Knight – b. 1782, bur. 12 Dec 1824 (Burial, **St. Luke Parish**)

Ransford Knight (deceased):

> **Residence - Brittain Street - Before December 12, 1824**
>
> **Age at Death - 42 years**

- Richard Knight – bur. 10 May 1717 (Burial, **St. Paul Parish**)

- Richard Knight – bur. 25 Mar 1767 (Burial, **St. James Parish**)

Richard Knight (deceased):

> **Residence - Dolphin's Barn - Before March 25, 1767**

- Richard Knight – b. 1784, bur. 10 Sep 1844 (Burial, **St. Mark Parish**)

Richard Knight (deceased):

>   Residence - Ring's End - Before September 10, 1844

>   Age at Death - 60 years

- Robert Knight – bur. 18 Dec 1707 (Burial, **St. Peter Parish**)

Robert Knight (deceased):

>   Residence - Kevin Street - Before December 18, 1707

- Robert Knight – bur. 30 Aug 1813 (Burial, **St. Mark Parish**)

Robert Knight (deceased):

>   Residence - Baggot Street - Before August 30, 1813

- Sabina Knight – bur. 23 Apr 1775 (Burial, **St. James Parish**)

Sabina Knight (deceased):

>   Residence - Copper Alley - Before April 23, 1775

- Samuel Knight – b. 1811, d. 2 May 1832, bur. 1832 (Burial, **Chapelizod Parish**)

Samuel Knight (deceased):

>   Residence - Chapelizod - May 2, 1832

>   Age at Death - 21 years

- Sarah Knight – b. 1631, bur. 2 Sep 1715 (Burial, **St. Werburgh Parish**)

Sarah Knight (deceased):

>   Residence - Gun Alley - Before September 2, 1715

>   Age at Death - 84 years

>   Cause of Death - age

- Sarah Knight – bur. 17 Jun 1811 (Burial, **St. Paul Parish**)

- Sarah Knight – b. 1802, d. 26 Feb 1873, bur. 1873 (Burial, **St. James Parish**)

Sarah Knight (deceased):

>   Residence - South Dublin Union - February 26, 1873

>   Age at Death - 71 years

Knight Surname Ireland: 1600s to 1900s

- Solomon Knight – bur. 18 Apr 1809 (Burial, **St. Paul Parish**)

- Sophia Knight – bur. 26 Dec 1840 (Burial, **St. Matthew Parish**)

Sophia Knight (deceased):

Residence - Ringsend - Before December 26, 1840

- Thomas Knight – bur. 12 Dec 1676 (Burial, **St. John Parish**)

- Thomas Knight – b. 1808, bur. 18 Mar 1844 (Burial, **St. Paul Parish**)

Thomas Knight (deceased):

Residence - Royal Barracks - Before March 18, 1844

Occupation - Private 5th Fusiliers - March 18, 1844

Age at Death - 36 years

- Unknown Knight (Mr.) – bur. 27 Feb 1684 (Burial, **St. John Parish**)

- Unknown Knight – bur. 29 Dec 1689 (Burial, **St. John Parish**)

Unknown Knight (deceased):

Relationship Status at Death - widow

- Unknown Knight – bur. 17 May 1702 (Burial, **St. Peter Parish**)

Unknown Knight (deceased):

Residence - Corkhill - Before May 17, 1702

- Unknown Knight – bur. 29 Mar 1703 (Burial, **St. Peter Parish**)

Unknown Knight (deceased):

Residence - Kevin's Port - Before March 29, 1703

- Unknown Knight – bur. 8 Jan 1714 (Burial, **St. Peter Parish**)

Unknown Knight (deceased):

Residence - Stephen's Green - Before January 8, 1714

- Unknown Knight – bur. 24 Apr 1735 (Burial, **St. Nicholas Without Parish**)

Unknown Knight (deceased):

Residence - St. Catherine's Parish - Before April 24, 1735

Hurst

- Unknown Knight – bur. 13 Apr 1738 (Burial, **St. Peter Parish**)

- Unknown Knight – bur. 31 Jan 1739 (Burial, **St. John Parish**)

- Unknown Knight – bur. 14 Sep 1758 (Burial, **St. Nicholas Without Parish**)

Unknown Knight (deceased):

    Residence - Patrick Street - Before September 14, 1758

- Unknown Knight (child) – bur. 16 Feb 1772 (Burial, **St. Mary Parish**)

Unknown Knight (deceased):

    Residence - Brittain Street - Before February 16, 1772

- Unknown Knight (Mr.) – bur. 2 Jan 1792 (Burial, **St. Paul Parish**)

- Unknown Knight (child) – bur. 26 Feb 1792 (Burial, **St. Audoen Parish**)

- Unknown Knight (Mrs.) – bur. 13 Feb 1803 (Burial, **St. Mary Parish**)

Unknown Knight (deceased):

    Residence - Henry Street - Before February 13, 1803

- Unknown Knight (Miss) – b. 1798, bur. 24 Jan 1838 (Burial, **St. Mary Parish**)

Unknown Knight (deceased):

    Residence - Jervis Street - Before January 24, 1838

    Age at Death - 40 years

- William Knight – bur. 14 Aug 1669 (Burial, **St. Michan Parish**)

William Knight (deceased):

    Occupation - Soldier of Sir John Stephen - Before August 14, 1669

- William Knight – b. 1656, bur. 29 May 1720 (Burial, **St. Werburgh Parish**)

William Knight (deceased):

    Residence - Gun Alley - Before May 29, 1720

    Age at Death - 64 years

    Cause of Death - consumption

- William Knight – bur. 28 Jun 1785 (Burial, **St. Audoen Parish**)

- William Knight – bur. 23 Nov 1805 (Burial, **St. Paul Parish**)

Knight Surname Ireland: 1600s to 1900s

- William Knight – bur. 8 Apr 1823 (Burial, **St. Mark Parish**)

- William Knight – b. 1760, bur. 22 Jan 1838 (Burial, **St. Mary Parish**)

William Knight (deceased):

    Residence - Simpson's Hospital - Before January 22, 1838

    Age at Death - 78 years

- William Knight – b. Jan 1845, bur. 12 Mar 1845 (Burial, **St. Paul Parish**)

William Knight (deceased):

    Residence - Richmond Barracks - Before March 12, 1845

    Age at Death - 3 months

    Remarks at Death - "Son of private Knight, 67th Foot."

- William Joseph Knight – b. 1864, bur. 24 May 1872 (Burial, **Arbour Hill Barracks Parish**)

William Joseph Knight (deceased):

    Residence - Island Bridge Barracks - May 24, 1872

    Age at Death - 8 years

- Wilt Knight – bur. 14 Jul 1690 (Burial, **St. John Parish**)

Individual Marriages

- Anne Knight & George Lambert McDonnell

  o Mary Anne Maria McDonnell – b. 17 Nov 1842, bapt. 9 Aug 1865 (Baptism, **St. Lawrence Parish** (RC))

George Lambert McDonnell (father):

Residence - 1 Jamieson Street, London - August 9, 1865

- Anne Knight & Gulielmo Connell

  o Anne Connell – b. 17 Mar 1870, bapt. 1 Apr 1870 (Baptism, **St. Lawrence Parish** (RC))

Gulielmo Connell (father):

Residence - 13 Church Road - April 1, 1870

- Anne Knight & John Grady – 7 Feb 1846 (Marriage, **Bandon Parish** (RC))

- Anne Knight & John Hughes

  o William Joseph Hughes – bapt. 1869 (Baptism, **St. Andrew Parish** (RC))

John Hughes (father):

Residence - 11 Lime Street - 1869

- Anne Knight, d. Before 2 Feb 1896 & John Riddall, d. Before 2 Feb 1896

  o John K. Riddall, b. 31 Oct 1842, bapt. 2 Feb 1896 (Baptism, **St. Mary, Pro Cathedral Parish** (RC)) & Elizabeth Kellagher – 2 Feb 1896 (Marriage, **St. Mary, Pro Cathedral Parish** (RC))

John K. Riddall (son):

Residence - Abbey Hotel - February 2, 1896

Elizabeth Kellagher, daughter of John Kellagher & Elizabeth Monaghan (daughter-in-law):

Residence - Abbey Hotel - February 2, 1896

John Kellagher (father):

Residence - Clones

- Anne Knight & Joseph Beard – 7 Apr 1782 (Marriage, **St. Nicholas Without Parish**)

Anne Knight (wife):

Occupation - Spinster - April 7, 1782

Joseph Beard (husband):

Occupation - Book Binder - April 7, 1782

- Anne Knight & Robert Elsin – 24 Jul 1631 (Marriage, **St. John Parish**)

- Anne Knight & William Campion (C a m p i o n) – 6 Jun 1819 (Marriage, **St. Luke Parish**)

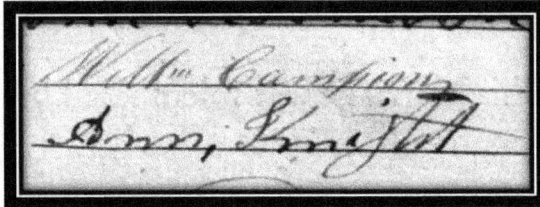

Signatures:

Anne Knight (wife):

Relationship Status at Marriage - widow

- Anne Knight & William Glannan (G l a n n a n)

  o James Glannan – bapt. 15 Jan 1772 (Baptism, **St. James Parish (RC)**)

- Betsy Jane Knight & William Henry Hatchings

  o Adelaide Hatchings – b. 1872, bapt. 1892 (Baptism, **St. Andrew Parish (RC)**)

William Henry Hatchings (father):

Residence - 1 Upper Merrion Street - 1892

- Bridget Knight & James Meagher

  o John Meagher – b. 22 Oct 1853, bapt. 24 Oct 1853 (Baptism, **St. Mary, Pro Cathedral Parish (RC)**)

Hurst

James Meagher (father):

Residence - 137 Capel Street - October 24, 1853

- Bridget Knight & James Rolls – 27 Dec 1842 (Marriage, **St. Andrew Parish (RC)**)

- Bridget Knight & Unknown Donnelly

  - Christopher Michael Donnelly – b. 1855, bapt. 1855 (Baptism, **Chapelizod Parish (RC)**)

Unknown Donnelly (father):

Residence - Chapelizod - 1855

- Bridget Anne Knight & James Maher – 22 Jan 1849 (Marriage, **St. Mary, Pro Cathedral Parish (RC)**)

  - Henry James Maher – b. 22 Jan 1855, bapt. 29 Jan 1855 (Baptism, **St. Mary, Pro Cathedral Parish (RC)**)

  - Mary Bridget Maher – b. 14 Aug 1856, bapt. 18 Aug 1856 (Baptism, **St. Mary, Pro Cathedral Parish (RC)**)

  - Hannah Maher – b. 27 Apr 1859, bapt. 29 Apr 1859 (Baptism, **St. Mary, Pro Cathedral Parish (RC)**)

  - Joseph Gulielmo Maher – b. 23 Jan 1861, bapt. 25 Jan 1861 (Baptism, **St. Mary, Pro Cathedral Parish (RC)**)

  - Teresa Maher – b. 2 Oct 1862, bapt. 3 Oct 1862 (Baptism, **St. Mary, Pro Cathedral Parish (RC)**)

James Maher (father):

Residence - 137 Capel Street - January 29, 1855

August 18, 1856

April 29, 1859

January 25, 1861

October 3, 1862

Knight Surname Ireland: 1600s to 1900s

- Catherine Knight & Edward Hannon (H a n n o n)

  o Daniel Hannon – bapt. Sep 1807 (Baptism, **St. Nicholas Parish (RC)**)

- Catherine Knight & John Jones – 11 Jun 1876 (Marriage, **St. Mary, Haddington Road Parish (RC)**)

- Catherine Knight & John Robinson – 15 Nov 1794 (Marriage, **St. Bride Parish**)

John Robinson (husband):
  Occupation - Lapedary - November 15, 1794

- Catherine Knight & Redmond McGrath – 11 Sep 1760 (Marriage, **St. Andrew Parish (RC)**)

- Eleanor Knight & Dennis Hayes – 6 Jul 1742 (Marriage, **St. Michan Parish (RC)**)

- Eleanor Knight & Michael Dunn

  o James Dunn – bapt. 26 Nov 1769 (Baptism, **St. Catherine Parish (RC)**)

- Elizabeth Knight & Gulielmo Hutchings

  o Adelaide Hutchings & Joseph Peake – 3 Nov 1897 (Marriage, **Chapelizod Parish (RC)**)

Adelaide Hutchings (daughter):
  Residence - Chapelizod - November 3, 1897

Joseph Peake, son of Thomas Peake & Catherine Keegan (son-in-law):
  Residence - Low Road, Knockmaroon - November 3, 1897

- Elizabeth Knight & James Stack

  o James Stack – bapt. 27 Nov 1835 (Baptism, **St. Catherine Parish (RC)**)

- Elizabeth Knight & James Stukey

  o Thomas Joseph Stukey – b. 4 May 1860, bapt. 25 Mar 1889 (Baptism, **St. Mary, Pro Cathedral Parish (RC)**)

Thomas Joseph Stukey (son):
  Residence - Alborough Barracks - March 25, 1889

Hurst

- Elizabeth Knight & John Drinan (D r i n a n)

  o Charles Drinan – b. 13 Mar 1834, bapt. 13 Mar 1834 (Baptism, **Killarney Parish** (RC))

  o Elizabeth Drinan – b. 21 May 1835, bapt. 21 May 1835 (Baptism, **Killarney Parish** (RC))

  o Mary Frances Drinan – b. 24 Sep 1837, bapt. 24 Sep 1837 (Baptism, **Killarney Parish** (RC))

  o John Drinan – bapt. 21 Feb 1843 (Baptism, **Douglas Parish** (RC))

John Drinan (father):

Residence - Killarney - March 13, 1834

Roseville - May 21, 1835

September 24, 1837

Ballyorbere - February 21, 1843

- Elizabeth Knight & John Henessy

  o John Henessy – bapt. 2 Apr 1828 (Baptism, **Cork - South Parish** (RC))

- Elizabeth Knight & John Mahoney

  o John Mahoney – bapt. 2 Jun 1880 (Baptism, **Innishannon Parish** (RC))

John Mahoney (father):

Residence - Lissinisky - June 2, 1880

- Elizabeth Knight & Joseph Burnam (B u r n a m) – 26 Sep 1694 (Marriage, **St. Andrew Parish**)

- Elizabeth Knight & Martin Sunderland

  o Arthur W. Sunderland & Margaret E. Galvin – 2 Jul 1902 (Marriage, **Killarney Parish** (RC))

Arthur W. Sunderland (son):

Residence - Waterville - July 2, 1902

Margaret E. Galvin, daughter of Timothy Galvin & Bridget A. Horan (daughter-in-law):

Residence - Waterville - July 2, 1902

Knight Surname Ireland: 1600s to 1900s

- Elizabeth Knight & Michael Kane

  o Matthew Kane – bapt. May 1851 (Baptism, **St. James Parish** (RC))

- Elizabeth Knight & Robert Preston – 1680 (Marriage, **St. Michael Parish**)

- Elizabeth Knight & Thomas Tylson – 6 Oct 1708 (Marriage, **St. Peter Parish**)

- Elizabeth Knight & William Kerney (K e r n e y)

  o Wilhelmina Kerney – bapt. 10 Feb 1832 (Baptism, **St. Catherine Parish** (RC))

- Elizabeth Knight & William Roche – 1 Mar 1832 (Marriage, **St. Andrew Parish** (RC))

  o Thomas Knight Roche – bapt. 1842 (Baptism, **St. Andrew Parish** (RC))

- Elizabeth Knight & William Smith – 25 Apr 1622 (Marriage, **St. John Parish**)

- Elizabeth Knight & William Smyth – 25 Feb 1622 (Marriage, **St. John Parish**)

- Ellen Knight & John Taylor – 2 May 1854 (Marriage, **Cork - SS. Peter & Paul Parish** (RC))

  o Mary Taylor – bapt. 27 Sep 1855 (Baptism, **Cork - South Parish** (RC))

  o William Taylor – bapt. 1 Feb 1857 (Baptism, **Cork - SS. Peter & Paul Parish** (RC))

  o Ellen Taylor – bapt. 29 Aug 1858 (Baptism, **Cork - SS. Peter & Paul Parish** (RC))

  o John Taylor – b. 17 May 1862, bapt. 25 May 1862 (Baptism, **Cork - SS. Peter & Paul Parish** (RC))

- Emma Knight & John Plumb

  o James Plumb – b. 29 Aug 1877, bapt. 21 Nov 1899 (Baptism, **Rathmines Parish** (RC))

John Plumb (father):

Residence - Bunling North, Hertfordshire - November 21, 1899

- Esther Knight & Michael Walsh

  o Elizabeth Walsh – bapt, 1837 (Baptism, **St. Mary, Haddington Road Parish** (RC))

- Hannah Knight & Charles Washington – 5 Nov 1786 (Marriage, **St. Michan Parish**)

Hurst

- Hannah Knight & James McCann – 17 Dec 1826 (Marriage, **Clontarf Parish**)

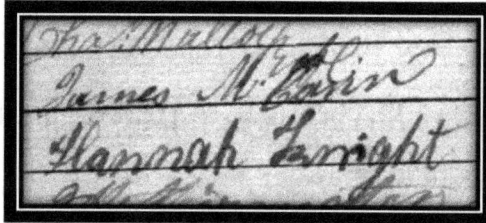

Signatures:

- Hannah Knight & William Connell – 2 Jul 1855 (Marriage, **Cork - South Parish (RC)**)

- Harriet Knight & George Calwell

  - Henry John Joseph Calwell – b. 1878, bapt. 1878 (Baptism, **St. Andrew Parish (RC)**)

George Calwell (father):

Residence - 20 City Quay - 1878

- Honora Knight John Cummins

  - Jane Cummins – bapt. 4 Jun 1843 (Baptism, **Kinsale Parish (RC)**)

  - Catherine Cummins – bapt. 17 May 1845 (Baptism, **Kinsale Parish (RC)**)

John Cummins (father):

Residence - Glen - June 4, 1843

May 17, 1845

- Honora Knight & John Gealagh

  - Julia Gealagh – bapt. 13 Jul 1815 (Baptism, **Ardfield & Rathbarry Parish (RC)**)

- Honora Knight & John Hely

  - Mary Hely – bapt. 24 Mar 1826 (Baptism, **Skibbereen (Creagh & Sullon) Parish (RC)**)

John Hely (father):

Residence - North Street - March 24, 1826

- Isabel Knight & Edward Doyle

  - Mary Anne Doyle – bapt. 11 Apr 1853 (Baptism, **St. Michan Parish (RC)**)

- Isabel Knight & Jonathan Curle – 23 Apr 1729 (Marriage, **St. Nicholas Without Parish**)

Knight Surname Ireland: 1600s to 1900s

- Jane Knight & Edward Pope – 10 Feb 1699 (Marriage, **St. Peter Parish**)

- Jane Knight & Henry Willis

  - Arthur Edwin Willis, b. 17 Mar 1867, bapt. 13 Feb 1889 (Baptism, **Rathmines Parish** (RC))

    & Catherine Moore – 4 Mar 1889 (Marriage, **Rathmines Parish** (RC))

Arthur Edwin Willis (son):

   Residence - Portobello Barrack - March 4, 1889

Catherine Moore, daughter of Patrick Moore & Mary Jones (daughter-in-law):

   Residence - 1 Beechwood Road - March 4, 1889

Henry Willis (father):

   Residence - Charles Street, Petersfield, Hampshire - February 13, 1889

- Jane Knight & John Sears – 14 Sep 1733 (Marriage, **Dingle Parish**)

Jane Knight (wife):

   Residence - Dingle - September 14, 1733

John Sears (husband):

   Residence - Killmalkeader - September 14, 1733

- Jane Knight & John Taylor – 19 May 1831 (Marriage, **St. Mark Parish**)

Signatures:

Wedding Witnesses:

Michael Singleton & Fain Knight

Signatures:

- Joyce Knight & Thomas Whitfield – 3 Feb 1667 (Marriage, **St. Michan Parish**)

- Julia Mary Teresa Knight & Richard Patrick Ingham

  o Mary Helen Teresa Ingham – b. 1897, bapt. 1897 (Baptism, **St. Andrew Parish (RC)**)

  o Richard Henry Joseph Ingham – b. 1898, bapt. 1898 (Baptism, **St. Andrew Parish (RC)**)

Richard Patrick Ingham (father):

Residence - 11 Upper Mount Street - 1897

1898

Knight Surname Ireland: 1600s to 1900s

- Margaret Knight & Joseph Jones

  o Lawrence John Jones – b. 14 Nov 1853, bapt. 18 Nov 1853 (Baptism, **St. Lawrence Parish (RC)**)

  o Bridget Jones – b. 18 Nov 1855, bapt. 19 Nov 1855 (Baptism, **St. Lawrence Parish (RC)**)

Joseph Jones (father):

  Residence - Nixon Street - November 18, 1853

  5 Cottage Place Newfoundland Street - November 19, 1855

- Margaret Knight & Michael Kinch – 4 Apr 1722 (Marriage, **St. Andrew Parish**)

- Margaret Knight & Thomas Burdell – 20 Nov 1676 (Marriage, **St. Michan Parish**)

- Margaret Knight & Thomas Gill – 26 Oct 1676 (Marriage, **St. Michan Parish**)

- Martha Knight & George Long

  o Joseph George Long – b. 6 Jan 1856, bapt. 22 Apr 1888 (Baptism, **Caherciveen Parish (RC)**)

George Knight (father):

  Residence - Caherciveen - April 22, 1888

- Martha Knight & Nicholas Bulger – 28 Aug 1763 (Marriage, **St. Catherine Parish (RC)**)

  o Charles Bulger – bapt. 5 Jul 1767 (Baptism, **St. James Parish (RC)**)

  o Bridget Bulger – bapt. 12 Nov 1769 (Baptism, **St. Catherine Parish (RC)**)

  o Andrew Bulger – bapt. 5 Dec 1779 (Baptism, **St. Catherine Parish (RC)**)

  o Richard Bulger – bapt. 23 Sep 1781 (Baptism, **St. Catherine Parish (RC)**)

  o Bridget Bulger – bapt. 6 Oct 1783 (Baptism, **St. Catherine Parish (RC)**)

- Mary Knight & John Carey

  o Bridget Christina Carey – b. 4 Jan 1883, bapt. 8 Jan 1883 (Baptism, **St. Mary, Pro Cathedral Parish (RC)**)

Hurst

John Carey (father):

Residence - 23 Summerhill - January 8, 1883

- Mary Knight & John Kearey

  - Josephine Mary Kearey – b. 30 Sep 1888, bapt. 3 Oct 1888 (Baptism, **St. Mary, Pro Cathedral Parish** (RC))

John Kearey (father):

Residence - 5 Rutland Place - October 3, 1888

- Mary Knight & John Kinsey

  - Bridget Anne Kinsey – b. 11 Nov 1892, bapt. 14 Nov 1892 (Baptism, **St. Mary, Pro Cathedral Parish** (RC))

John Kinsey (father):

Residence - 5 Rutland Row - November 14, 1892

- Mary Knight & John McDermott (M c D e r m o t t)

  - William McDermott – bapt. 27 Aug 1786 (Baptism, **St. Michan Parish** (RC))

  - Edward McDermott – bapt. 29 Jul 1789 (Baptism, **St. Michan Parish** (RC))

- Mary Knight & Mark Cooney

  - Hannah Cooney – bapt. 18 Jul 1824 (Baptism, **Cork - South Parish** (RC))

  - Hannah Cooney – bapt. 13 Nov 1826 (Baptism, **Cork - South Parish** (RC))

  - Mark Cooney – bapt. 30 Jan 1830 (Baptism, **Cork - South Parish** (RC))

- Mary Knight & Michael Crawly – 16 Apr 1789 (Marriage, **St. Michan Parish** (RC))

- Mary Knight & Peter Ryan – 9 Jul 1820 (Marriage, **St. Andrew Parish** (RC))

- Mary Knight & Thomas Balfe – 24 Oct 1767 (Marriage, **St. Catherine Parish** (RC))

- Mary Knight & Thomas Nall

  - Ellen Nall – b. 6 Sep 1896, bapt. 14 Sep 1896 (Baptism, **St. Mary, Pro Cathedral Parish** (RC))

Knight Surname Ireland: 1600s to 1900s

Thomas Nall (father):

Residence - 39 Bucking Builds - September 14, 1896

- Mary Knight & William Read – 12 Jul 1825 (Marriage, **St. Peter Parish**)

Mary Knight (wife):

Occupation - Spinster - July 12, 1825

William Read (husband):

Residence - St. Andrew's Parish - July 12, 1825

- Mary Anne Knight & Charles Reardon – Jul 1832 (Marriage, **Cork - South Parish (RC)**)

- Mary Anne Knight & John Lyons – 26 Jan 1856 (Baptism, **Cork - SS. Peter & Paul Parish (RC)**)

  - Daniel Lyons – bapt. 15 Feb 1857 (Baptism, **Cork - SS. Peter & Paul Parish (RC)**)

  - Mary Lyons – bapt. 1 Apr 1868 (Baptism, **Cork - South Parish (RC)**)

  - John Lyons – bapt. 3 Jan 1870 (Baptism, **Cork - South Parish (RC)**)

- Mary Anne Taunton Knight & Philip Lawless

  - Philip Barry Lawless – bapt. 1 Jul 1851 (Baptism, **St. Mary, Pro Cathedral Parish (RC)**)

  - Teresa Mary Josephine Lawless – b. 7 Aug 1854, bapt. 8 Aug 1854 (Baptism, **St. Mary, Pro Cathedral Parish (RC)**)

  - Philippa Mary Josephine Lawless – b. 5 May 1856, bapt. 10 May 1856 (Baptism, **St. Mary, Pro Cathedral Parish (RC)**)

  - Jane Mary Josephine Lawless – b. 26 Nov 1857, bapt. 28 Nov 1857 (Baptism, **St. Mary, Pro Cathedral Parish (RC)**)

  - Philip Charles Lawless – b. 1860, bapt. 1860 (Baptism, **Sandyford Parish (RC)**)

Hurst

Philip Lawless (father):

Residence - 4 Mountjoy Square East - August 8, 1854

26 Mountjoy Square - May 10, 1856

20 Mountjoy Square - November 28, 1857

Kilgobbin - 1860

- Rebecca Knight & Joseph Ray – 12 Sep 1713 (Marriage, **St. Andrew Parish**)

- Sarah Knight & Abraham Loddell

  o Elizabeth Loddell – bapt. 14 Feb 1831 (Baptism, **St. Nicholas Parish (RC)**)

- Sarah Knight & Abraham Mardell

  o Joseph Mardell – bapt. 23 Jun 1811 (Baptism, **SS. Michael & John Parish (RC)**)

- Sarah Knight & Abraham Nordle

  o Patrick Joseph Nordle – bapt. 4 Mar 1820 (Baptism, **SS. Michael & John Parish (RC)**)

- Sarah Knight & Edward Fitzgerald

  o Edward Fitzgerald – bapt. 14 Jan 1781 (Baptism, **St. Catherine Parish (RC)**)

  o Anne Fitzgerald – bapt. 6 Apr 1783 (Baptism, **St. Catherine Parish (RC)**)

- Sarah Knight & Jeremiah Dwyer

  o Margaret Dwyer – bapt. 30 Jun 1844 (Baptism, **Cork - SS. Peter & Paul Parish (RC)**)

  o Mary Dwyer – bapt. 26 Apr 1846 (Baptism, **Cork - SS. Peter & Paul Parish (RC)**)

  o Sarah Dwyer – bapt. 4 Dec 1851 (Baptism, **Cork - SS. Peter & Paul Parish (RC)**)

  o Elizabeth Dwyer – bapt. 21 Mar 1853 (Baptism, **Cork - SS. Peter & Paul Parish (RC)**)

- Sarah Knight & John Donogan

  o Elizabeth Donogan – bapt. 8 May 1803 (Baptism, **Cork - South Parish (RC)**)

John Donogan (father):

Residence - Near Duglas - May 8, 1803

Knight Surname Ireland: 1600s to 1900s

- Sarah Knight & Patrick Fottrell

  o John Fottrell – bapt. 28 Apr 1847 (Baptism, **St. Michan Parish (RC)**)

  o Joseph Fottrell – bapt. 25 Nov 1850 (Baptism, **St. Michan Parish (RC)**)

  o Patrick Fottrell – b. 9 Mar 1854, bapt. 20 Mar 1854 (Baptism, **St. Mary, Pro Cathedral Parish (RC)**)

  o Sarah Anne Fottrell – b. 17 Aug 1859, bapt. 24 Aug 1859 (Baptism, **St. Mary, Pro Cathedral Parish (RC)**)

  o Gulielmo Fottrell – b. 31 Oct 1861, bapt. 6 Nov 1861 (Baptism, **St. Mary, Pro Cathedral Parish (RC)**)

Patrick Fottrell (father):

   Residence - 35 Upper Abbey Street - March 20, 1854

   August 24, 1859

   Britain Street, Rotunda - November 6, 1861

- Sarah Knight & Thomas Tucker

  o Edward Tucker – bapt. 1775 (Baptism, **SS. Michael & John Parish (RC)**)

- Sophia Knight & Richard Heyday – 6 Apr 1817 (Marriage, **St. Werburgh Parish**)

- Sophia Knight & Thomas Whelan

  o John Joseph Whelan – b. 15 Aug 1884, bapt. 30 Oct 1884 (Baptism, **St. Audoen Parish (RC)**)

  o Michael Patrick Whelan – b. 15 Aug 1884, bapt. 30 Oct 1884 (Baptism, **St. Audoen Parish (RC)**)

  o Mary Josephine Whelan – b. 1887, bapt. 8 Feb 1887 (Baptism, **St. Audoen Parish (RC)**)

Thomas Whelan (father):

   Residence - 6 Cook Street - October 30, 1884

   February 8, 1887

Hurst

- Susan Knight & Cologh McMahone – 19 Apr 1640 (Marriage, **St. John Parish**)

- Susannah Knight & Robert Oliver – 6 Nov 1705 (Marriage, **St. Peter Parish**)

- Susannah Knight & Thomas Brodhurst – 23 May 1659 (Marriage, **St. Bride Parish**)

- Susannah Knight & William Barlow – 30 Jul 1693 (Marriage, **St. Michan Parish**)

Name Variations

Includes Latin and Abbreviated forms of names found in the original documents.

Abigail = Abigale, Abigall

Anne = Ann, Anna, Annae

Bartholomew = Barth, Bartholmeus, Bartholomeo

Bridget = Birgis, Brigid, Brigida, Bridgit

Catherine = Catharine, Catharina, Catharinae, Catherina, Cath, Catha, Cathae, Cathe, Cathn

Charles = Carolus, Charls, Chas

Christopher = Christoph

Daniel = Danielem, Danielis

Edmund = Edmond

Edward = Ed, Edwd

Eleanor = Eleo, Eleonora, Elinor, Ellenor

Elizabeth = Betty, Elisa, Elisabeth, Eliz, Eliza, Elizab, Elizh, Elizth

Ellen = Elena, Ellena

Emily= Emilia

Esther = Essie, Ester

Frances = Fannie, Fanny

Francis = Fransicum

George = Geo, Georg, Georgius

Grace = Gratiae

Gulielmo = Guil, Guillelmi, Gulielmum, Guillelmus, Gulmi

Knight Surname Ireland: 1600s to 1900s

Harold = Harry

Helen = Helena

Honor = Hanora, Honora

James = Jacobi, Jacobus, Jas

Jane = Joanna

Jeanne = Jeannae, Joannae

Joan = Johanna, Joney

John = Jno, Joannem, Joannes, Johannis

Joseph = Jos

Juliana = Julian

Leticia = Letitia, Lettice, Letticia

Margaret = Margarita, Margaritae, Margeret, Marget, Margt

Mary = Maria, My

Mary Anne = Marianna, Marianne, Maryanne

Michael = Michaelis, Michl

Patrick = Pat, Patt, Patk, Patricii, Patricius

Peter = Petri

Richard = Ricardi, Ricardus, Rich, Richd

Robert = Roberti

Rose = Rosa, Rosae

Samuel = Samuelis

Thomas = Thom, Thomae, Thoms, Thos, Ths

Timothy = Timotheus, Timy

William = Wil, Will, Willm, Wm

Notes

Notes

Notes

Notes

Notes

Notes

Index

C

F

G

H

Knight Surname Ireland: 1600s to 1900s

Hurst

Knight Surname Ireland: 1600s to 1900s

Knight Surname Ireland: 1600s to 1900s

Hurst

Y

About The Author

Donovan Hurst graduated from San Diego State University with a Bachelor of Arts in the major field of studies of History and a minor in the field of studies of Anthropology. He is a current member of The General Society of Mayflower Descendants and has been conducting genealogical research for over 10 years tracing back his ancestors to their ancestral homelands in Denmark, England, France, Germany, Ireland, Norway, and Scotland.

www.ingramcontent.com/pod-product-compliance
Lightning Source LLC
Chambersburg PA
CBHW080333270326
41927CB00014B/3197